This Book Is Given to

Jake Cassell

By

The Popowski Family

In Recognition of His Completion of the Eagle Scout
Badge

D1113257

4|2|2017

1

Dare to Soar

A Gift, and a Challenge, to the Eagle Scout

Thomas Mercaldo

Printed in the United States.
First Printing
Paperback Edition

Aquinas Scout Books
c/o Thomas C. Mercaldo
154 Herbert Street
Milford, CT 06461
(203) 876-2822

Contact us by email at: BoyScoutBooks@aol.com

Aquinas Scout Fun Books is not officially affiliated with the Boy Scouts of America, Girl Scouts of America. Scouts Canada or the World Organization of Scouting.

ISBN - 13: 978-1534955783
ISBN - 10: 153495578X

This book is dedicated to those Eagle Scouts who desire to serve others and pursue excellence in everything they do.

Contents

Introduction

Congratulations on receiving your Eagle Scout Award. This is a great honor and a great achievement. This is a book written for the new Eagle Scout. It contains all kinds of information about the Eagle Scout Award, but most importantly, this book offers the new Eagle Scout a challenge to fulfill the promise of the Eagle Scout badge.

Since Scouting began in the United States in 1910, only 1.8% of the boys who have joined Scouting have gone on to achieve the rank of Eagle Scout. While this number has fluctuated over the years from a low of 0% in 1910 and a high of nearly 5% in other years, the Eagle Scout Award remains the most recognized symbol of accomplishment in any youth organization. Had Robert Baden-Powell, the founder of Scouting, had his way, however, this would not have been the case.

Robert Baden-Powell introduced the concept of badges for achievements in his 1908 best-selling book Scouting for Boys. Initially, the highest available rank for Scouting in the United States was to be the "Wolf Badge," based on the Silver Wolf badge in Great Britain. However, when the draft version of the Handbook for Boys was circulated among the early American Scouting leaders in June of 1911, many thought the highest award should more appropriately recognize the American eagle. No Wolf rank was ever awarded and when the final version of the Boy Scout Handbook was published in August of 1911. The highest rank in Scouting in the United States was dubbed "Eagle Scout."

The original Eagle badge design illustrated in the handbook showed an eagle in flight, but the design was changed to the current design before any Eagle Scout badges were issued. The first Eagle Scout medal was awarded to Arthur Rose Eldred, a 17 year old Scout from Troop 1 in Rockville Centre, New York (Long Island). In 1982, thirteen year old Alexander Holsinger of Normal, Illinois was recognized as the one millionth Eagle Scout. The Eagle Scout badge has been awarded on average a little more than 17,000 times per year. Less than one-half of one percent of men born in America receive this award.

Dare to Soar

Dare to Soar: A Challenge to Fulfill the Promise of the Eagle Scout

Congratulations! You are an Eagle Scout. You started down a lengthy trail a long time ago. You have carried a heavy pack. You have climbed a steep hill. You have run a long race and you have finished strong. You started this race with many by your side. Today, you stand among a select few.

You should be proud of your accomplishment, and you will probably remember the day you received your Eagle Award for the rest of your life. But in reality, the day you got the Eagle Scout Award is not the day to remember. This award was the culmination of many days effort over a period of years, and it is these days, and the work that was done along the way to prepare you for this day, that should be cherished and remembered.

Now it is time for you to start a new journey, a journey along life's trail as an Eagle Scout. You have achieved a place of honor, but you now also have a new responsibility, a responsibility to strive for greatness. As an Eagle, you are challenged to become the best person that you can be. You are not called to wallow with the swine or to swim with the fish. As an Eagle you are called to soar above the clouds. **Dare to soar**.

Dare to Soar. This is the challenge to the new Eagle Scout. This may sound like a simple challenge, but it is not. Many will push this challenge aside. For some, the Eagle Scout badge will be their crowning achievement and for others this award simply marks the start of lifelong journey of accomplishment. Dare not to push the Eagle Scout challenge aside, but to accept it, and to continue down the road to greatness. **Dare to read on.**

Do you want to live a life filled with happiness, excitement and accomplishment? Do you want to be part of bringing change to the world? Do you want to wake up every morning energized at the thought of doing something interesting; something meaningful, something truly important? Do you want to put the gifts God has given you to the greatest possible use? Do you dare to develop your skills and abilities to the fullest? Do you **Dare to soar**?

As an Eagle Scout you may feel you have already accepted the challenge to be the best person you can be. However, the Dare to Soar is to accept an even greater challenge. The challenge to be one of the bold few who will face life courageously ready to strike out anything that is keeping you from being your best. To stop accepting whatever happens and instead create a destiny of your choosing. When you Dare to Soar you will have a great power at your disposal that you never had before. Your life and your every action will take on new significance.

Be prepared. Do a good turn daily. You have heard the Scout slogan and motto before. You are also familiar with the words of the Scout Oath:

On my honor I will do my best to do my duty to God and my Country and to obey the Scout Law. To help other people at all times, to keep myself physically strong, mentally awake and morally straight.

And the Law:

A Scout is Trustworthy, Loyal, Helpful, Friendly, Courteous, Kind, Obedient, Cheerful, Thrifty, Brave, Clean, and Reverent.

You know these words well, and you are well served to live your life dedicated to following them. The Dare to Soar challenge asks you to look at these commitments in a new way. Daring to Soar means accepting the below challenges that these pledges offer us:

The Eagle Scout Challenge
The 8 Dares of the Eagle Scout -
The Dares of Achieving Greatness:

1. Dare to Have a Positive Attitude

2. Dare to Do Your Best

3. Dare to Be a Genius

4. Dare to Be Physically Strong.

5. Dare to Have Courage

6. Dare to Be a Person of Great Character

7. Dare to Have Charisma

8. Dare to Give to Others

As an Eagle Scout you are challenged to accept these 8 Dares. To live life in accordance with the Scout Oath, Law, Motto and Slogan by making these traits — that are in essence the fulfillment of the oath and law — a part of you. To build a life not just filled with goodness but greatness.

Perhaps you believe that greatness is not possible for you. Perhaps you feel that you are not capable of soaring. **You can soar!**

You have what it takes or you could not have become an Eagle Scout. To soar, all you need is a can-do attitude of service to others. This approach backstopped with preparation, (the next merit badges of life), will enable you not only to get off the ground but to soar above the clouds.

Your attitude will be the biggest factor in dictating whether or not you soar. The first of the 8 great Eagle Scout Dares is to develop a positive can-do attitude.

Chapter 1

Dare to Have a Positive Attitude

When asked to name the most important of the Scout Laws, few would begin by listing "cheerful." Yet, being cheerful and having the right attitude is generally the most important factor required to achieve

> "In order to succeed, we must first believe we can."
> – Michael Korda

greatness. In order to succeed, you must first believe you can. If you think you can, you can. If you think you can't, you're right. Attitude is more important than the past, than education, than money, than circumstances; it is more important than intelligence appearance, skill or ability. Attitude will determine the success of a business, family or Scout Troop. The

> "If you think you can, you can. If you think you can't, you're right."
> – Mary Kay Ash

amazing thing is, attitude is the one thing you have the ability to control every day. You cannot change the past; you cannot make others act in a particular way. You do, however, have control over the single most important factor influencing your happiness and success, and that factor is your attitude.

What makes a good attitude? A good attitude means believing in yourself and believing in others. It means you are focused on the positives. It means you do your best. Having a good attitude means you approach life's challenges with enthusiasm and optimism. In many respects, success in any situation is simply attitude over obstacles. When a pessimistic person runs into obstacles, they give up. When an optimistic person runs into obstacles, they try harder. Only those that can overcome adversity can be truly successful, and only the optimist is ready to overcome adversity. You only need to look at your attitude to know whether or not you ultimately will experience success.

> "The only disability in life is a bad attitude."

At a recent Camporee, I asked a Scout what was the most important day of his life. His answer was most surprising. "Let me tell you," he said. "Recently, I went to have my handwriting analyzed and I learned that I was an extrovert. All my life, I have been timid and shy, with a huge inferiority complex. But all that has changed these last few weeks, and I've been having a great time."

I have known this Scout for many years, and he has become like a new person. Yet really, there is only one thing about him that has changed, and that is his attitude. He became confident and began to believe in himself, because someone told him that is the way he is supposed to be. Someone else needed to believe

15

in him, before he could believe in himself. Don't limit yourself by the expectations of others. Don't be who others want you to be, be the person you dream to become! Most importantly, don't wait for others to believe in you, believe in yourself. You can become whoever you want to be, if you only you have the right attitude and believe in yourself!

But having a good attitude is more than just having self-confidence. Many confident people fail. Over-confidence in fact is an obstacle to attaining your goals. A good attitude means not only believing in yourself, but following up this belief with action. To put it another way, to have a good attitude and to soar you must also demonstrate a strong work ethic.

Many would consider cellist Pablo Casals a success. World renowned for his unique abilities, at the age of 80 Pablo Casals kept practicing his instrument for four to five hours every day. Someone once asked him, why, at his age, he still worked so hard. "Because," he said, "I have a notion that I am making some progress." More than ability, it was his attitude that made Pablo Casals a success, and it was his attitude that sustained him throughout his life.

Chapter 2

Dare to Do Your Best

Determination is the result of possessing a strong work ethic. The harder you work the harder it is to surrender. When you put your whole self into what you do, giving up is no longer an option. Some of the world's greatest feats were accomplished by people not smart enough to know they were impossible.

There once was a man who just didn't know when to give up. He was a perennial loser. Here's what happened to him at various times in his life. At the age of:

22, he failed in business, at
23, he ran for legislature and was defeated, at
24, he again failed in business, at
25, he was elected to the legislature, at
26, his sweetheart died, at
27, he had a nervous breakdown, at
29, he was defeated for Speaker, at
31, he was defeated for Elector, at
34, he was defeated for Congress, at
39, he was defeated for Congress, at
46, he was defeated for the Senate, at
47, he was defeated for Vice-President, at
49, he was defeated for the Senate, at

51, he was elected President of the United States.

That's the record of Abraham Lincoln. Some might say he was a perennial loser; others however know he was a winner and a great American. Sometimes life offers us more defeats than victories. It is how we respond to those defeats that shapes who we are. Abraham Lincoln never gave up. He believed in himself and his ideas, and he never stopped working hard. Hard work yields results.

> **Don't Give Up**
> "Inside of a ring or out, ain't nothing wrong with going down. It's staying down that's wrong."
> – Muhammad Ali

Lincoln understood that being defeated is only a temporary condition. Giving up is the only thing that can make defeat permanent. Don't ever allow yourself to give up! Muhammad Ali, the only three time world heavyweight boxing champion took his defeats with grace and with a sense of renewed determination. He once said, "Inside of a ring or out, ain't nothing wrong with going down. It's staying down that's wrong."

Persistence

"There was a judge in a certain town who did not fear God and did not respect man. Now there was a certain widow in that town and she kept coming to this judge saying, "Do me justice against my adversary." And he would not for a long time. But after a while he said to himself, "Although I do not fear God nor even respect man, yet because this widow bothers me, I will do her justice, lest by her continual coming she finally wears me out."

-Luke 18:1-5

Many times in life we are faced with challenges where we fail the first time. Often the key to success comes in working hard, trying again, and staying with things. Be persistent in your pursuit of things that are important, and through your continued effort you will find success. Success is out there waiting for you if you just do the right things every day.

Louis Pasteur was one of the greatest benefactors of all humanity. He solved the mysteries of rabies, anthrax, cholera and silkworm diseases and he contributed to the development of the first vaccines. Pasteur was once asked where his genius derived from and his answer was most telling. He replied, "Let me tell you the secret that has led me to my goal. My strength lies solely in my tenacity."

> "Fall seven times,
> stand up eight."
> – Japanese Proverb

Success is more a matter of persistence than a question of innate ability. It requires common sense much more than it demands genius. Success is the result of preparation and hard work. It is learning from our mistakes, and not being afraid to try again. There are no great secrets that will lead you to be a success. It is out there waiting for you if you just do the right things, and take steps toward your goals, every single day.

During World War II, Great Britain faced what seemed impossible odds. Undermanned and under equipped, the Royal Air Force attempted to fend off relentless air attacks from Axis nations in the Battle of Britain. With their air force depleted, London was devastated by a series of nighttime terror bombings that were designed to break the morale of the British people. Hitler believed Churchill would succumb to pressure to enter into a peace treaty. But Churchill refused to give up. On October 29, 1941, speaking to a group of young men in England, Churchill uttered these words, "Never give in, never give in, never, never, never, never—in nothing, great or small, large or petty—never give in except to convictions of honor and good sense." Churchill's stand against Hitler ultimately allowed the allies to launch an attack from Britain to retake Europe. His determination against seemingly impossible odds changed the trajectory of the war.

Albert Einstein is considered by many to be the greatest thinker of the 20th century. Einstein did not however, believe that his genius was in any way a result of any special abilities that he had. "I know perfectly well that I myself have no special talents," he wrote. "It was curiosity, obsession, and sheer perseverance that brought me to my ideas." **Dare to live a life of determination!**

Don't give up
"You may have to fight a battle more than once to win it."
- Margaret Thatcher

Chapter 3

Dare to Be a Genius

Just as Einstein felt his brainpower was the result of hard work, famed 18th century intellect, historian and social writer Thomas Carlyle once said, "Genius is an infinite capacity for hard work." Intellect is created by exercising the mind. It is a result of a journey of discovery, a journey that includes reading and contemplation. Just as a boxer trains for a fight, to soar you must train your mind by reading the right kinds of books that will stimulate your mind. There is a correlation between reading and IQ. On average the more a person reads, the higher their IQ.

Recently, I spoke with a friend of mine who is a cable news reporter. He had opinions on nearly every topic. However, when I asked him why he had the opinions he had he couldn't support any of his views. This person read the news to others every day, but he let his writers tell him what to say and what to think. **Dare to think for yourself!**

Understand the details before forming your opinions. Don't read the Cliff Notes and then flatter yourself into thinking you understand Shakespeare.

Don't read a movie review and decide that you don't need to see it. We live in a fast paced society and these are the temptations the average person faces average day. **Dare not to be average! Dare to think for yourself!**

Thinking for yourself may not be as easy as it sounds. There are many obstacles to independent thinking and the biggest of these might be fear. Fear of what others will think of you for not conforming to their point of view. Fear of disagreeing with others, "rocking the boat", not fitting in. A free thinker bases their self-worth on something other than what people think of them. Free thinkers may experience rejection, discomfort and anguish, but they have learned to overlook these feelings in order to pursue what is right and true.

> **Steps to Thinking For Yourself:**
>
> 1. Stop being concerned what others think of you and your ideas.
> 2. Ask questions.
> 3. Consider motives.
> 4. Assume nothing.
> 5. Conduct research. Read. Learn.
> 6. Understand what you don't know.

Thinking for yourself also requires asking questions, particularly asking the question: "Why?" When you get an answer, don't accept it at face value, ask yourself, does this answer make sense? Try to think of exceptions, and ask yourself why those exceptions exist. Never be satisfied with answers that have many exceptions. Look for answers with few exceptions. Look for universal truths.

Consider motives. Often, people want others to think a certain way because this thinking benefits them in some way. That benefit is not always obvious or direct. Many times, people want you to adopt their viewpoint simply because it makes them feel more comfortable and secure (safety in numbers). Sometimes, people's beliefs make it easier for them to feel like a good person. When soliciting the views of others try and remember these factors may have greatly skewed their thinking. Don't be swayed by selfish or misguided motives; try to discover the truth whether it makes you feel comfortable or not.

Don't make any assumptions. Perhaps the biggest mistake even scientists make is the failure to question generally accepted facts and principles. For many years it was believed that ulcers were caused by a combination of factors that included poor diet and stress. That was until Barry Marshall and Robin Warren failed to accept this generally accepted principle and started to treat ulcers with antibiotics. Their work was ridiculed by other members of the medical community for more than 10 years, but today the antibiotic treatments they recommended have become the standard approach for treating ulcers throughout the world. Marshall and Robin did not accept what others had told them. They were not afraid of what others thought of them. Because of their courage, ulcers are now an easily treatable medical condition.

It's easier to accept what you hear than to do your own research and question what you hear. But to be a truly independent thinker you must conduct your own research and examine what you hear. You will be amazed at how many times you'll find evidence to contradict the statements you hear on the news or read in the newspaper. These "experts" spout erroneous information and never question the accuracy or truth of what they're saying. And if this is true of the "experts," it is even more common among the people you speak with each and every day. When you do your research, never accept something as a fact that you find from a single source or on a website. Many of the facts you read on the internet are simply not true. Look for opinions from reputable sources and seek data from people offering alternative points of view. Don't limit your research to those with similar perspectives; rather, challenge your viewpoint by seeking those with an opposite point of view.

Finally, to become an independent thinker you need to understand what you don't know. How do you gain an understanding of what you don't know? The best way to understand the limitations of your knowledge on any subject is to become an expert on a subject. Dare to be expert at something! Make a decision to pursue knowledge in an area that interests you and know this subject better than anyone else. Having expert knowledge in just one area will help you understand not just what you know, but what you don't know about topics. It will give you a reference point from which to measure subjects that you know little about. It will help you become above average.

In one way you have already proven you are not average. As an Eagle Scout you are a member of an exclusive club that only few make it into. But I ask, will attaining the Eagle Scout badge be your crowning achievement, or does something even greater await you? Every day while crossing the ocean, flying fish leap out of the water into the sunlight for a matter of seconds before falling back into the dark sea. Did you come all this way only to plunge back into darkness? Or did you just make a permanent leap into the light and warmth of the sun? I ask you, "Are you a flying fish, or an eagle?"

You can easily be a genius if you only understand what genius truly is. I once felt that I could never be a genius, but now I know that I possess a kind of genius that few have. I am a genius, in much the same way as that Coyote that chases the roadrunner is a genius. Sure the Coyote has had his share of spectacular failures, but it is in his failures that we gain exposure to his genius. The coyote thinks for himself. He dares to have creative ideas. He believes in his ideas and he puts these ideas into practice. He works hard and never gives up. He is not afraid to make mistakes. In many respects this is a definition of genius. Look at all the great thinkers Da Vinci, Einstein, Edison and Pasteur and they all demonstrated these traits. And it is in these traits, not their intellect, which made them geniuses.

So I dare to suggest that genius is the result of independent thinking, creativity, self-confidence, determination, hard work, and a willingness to make mistakes. These are skills anybody can have. You don't need to try to become a genius, simply demonstrate these traits in your daily life and you will exhibit genius without trying.

Many people are surprised to hear me say that a genius is willing to make mistakes. After all, shouldn't a genius not make mistakes? The truth is, it took Edison more than 1,000 tries before he developed a filament that would actually work inside a light bulb. Edison made a lot of mistakes. Today, few talk about Edison's failures; generally folks just marvel at his successes. My life took a sudden change the day I stopped taking myself too seriously and became willing to take risks and make mistakes. Once you are willing to take risks and are no longer afraid to make mistakes good things will happen. And there is in fact a kind of genius that comes when you are no longer concerned with what others think of your ideas and you are willing to try things that you believe in. Sure you may have some failures, but ultimately you will also experience great successes.

There is a genius inside you waiting to come out. But even if you are unwilling to embrace the genius inside you, you can use the same strategies as Einstein and Edison to harness the power of your creative mind and better manage your future. Here are some of the strategies they employed:

1. Look at problems in a new way.

Einstein brought creative thinking to problem solving by looking at problems in many different ways and finding perspectives that others had not taken. He took a fresh look at problems by restating them in new ways. Often, our first way of looking at problems is too biased towards our usual way of seeing things. It is in looking at a problem in different ways that we come to truly understand it.

2. Draw pictures! Geniuses make their thoughts visible.

Leonardo Da Vinci found it necessary to formulate his subject in as many different ways as possible in order to find solutions to the challenges he faced. He used art and the process of drawing pictures and diagrams from a variety of angles to stimulate his mind's creativity. This process brought information into a part of his brain that could not be reached through conversation or contemplation. Galileo was also noted for using this technique.

3. Set goals and produce.

Einstein published more than 200 papers. Shakespeare wrote 38 plays. Mozart produced more than 600 pieces of music. Edison held more than 1,000 patents. He set goals for the number of ideas he and his assistants needed to come up with, and he worked until he hit his quotas. Most great thinkers produce not only great works but also develop many "bad" ideas. What makes them great is that they weren't afraid to fail. Most people talk about Henry Ford as the genius who revolutionized the automobile industry. Few talk about the fact that the first three companies he started failed.

> "Most people fail in life not because they aim too high and miss. Most people fail in life because they aim too low and hit!"
> - Les Brown

4. Think in pairs. Think in extremes. Consider polar opposites.

Picasso believed that "every act of creation is first an act of destruction." Einstein imagined light as simultaneously a wave — like a wave in the water, and a particle. This theory lead him to a Nobel Prize for Physics in 1921. Physicist Niels Bohr believed that if you held opposites together, then you suspend your thought, and your mind moves to a new level.

Suspending thought (logic) may allow your mind to create a new form. Here are some questions that can help lead you to looking at problems in a new way:

A. What would happen if you did something?
B. What would happen if you didn't?
C. What wouldn't happen if you did?
D. What wouldn't happen if you didn't?

5. Pursue knowledge of diverse topics.

Generate a basic understanding of many subjects. Read. Attend college and learn not just about an area of specialization but undertake general studies in many disciplines. Be in a position to apply concepts from one discipline to another. Dare to be prepared.

Leonardo Da Vinci, Ben Franklin, Isaac Newtown, Galileo Galilei, Thomas Edison. Try to categorize any of these men and you will find it quite difficult. Each came to prominence in multiple disciplines. Were they scientists, inventors, businessmen, philosophers or mathematicians? Each had general knowledge in a variety of subjects and came to prominence for achievements in multiple disciplines. Sometimes the best way to understand one subject is to be the master of another.

6. Make novel combinations. Force relationships. Make connections between dissimilar subjects.

Coalesce thoughts, ideas and images into different combinations no matter how incongruent or unusual. Many great discoveries and inventions have come from making connections between dissimilar subjects. Samuel Morse, after seeing relay stations for the Pony Express, solved the telegraph signal strength problem he faced by inventing relay stations for telegraphic signals. Sir Isaac Newton tied together concepts from astronomy and physics. He used a new mathematical concept, fluxions (calculus), to illustrate these concepts and to explain his laws of motion. Grego Mendel combined mathematics and biology to create a new science, genetics. Leonardo Da Vinci imagined a relationship between the waves created by a stone hitting water and the sound of a bell. This led him to realize that sound travels in waves. Newton make a connection between the way an apple falls to the ground to the way planets move around the sun.

7. Think metaphorically and anti-metaphorically.

The concept here is to create new understanding by using metaphors and figures of speech. Take a word or phrase used to describe one thing and ascribe it to another. This process helps the mind create connections and better conceptual understandings. Aristotle considered metaphor a sign of true genius, and he believed that the individual who had the capacity to perceive resemblances between separate areas of existence and link them together was a person of special ability.

8. **Be prepared** for chance happenings.

Whenever we attempt to do something and fail, in effect we end up doing something else. This something else is a creative accident. We may ask ourselves why we have failed to do what we set out to, but the creative accident provokes a different question. What have we done? Failure can be productive only if we do not focus on it as an unproductive result. Instead analyze the process, its components, and how we can change these to arrive at some other result.

Alexander Fleming had such an experience when he was growing staphylococcus cultures. He observed that one culture had been contaminated by a blue-green mold and that colonies of bacteria adjacent to the mold were being dissolved. This creative accident coupled with Fleming's curiosity and ability to ask the right questions lead to the discovery of penicillin.

The above techniques are not difficult and can be useful when looking at any problem. You can expand the capacity of your mind to solve problems by using these techniques. In effect, you can train yourself to think like a genius. No, you may not have the world's highest IQ, but if you take your experiences and think about them in the right way, you can accomplish great things. You can create intellect by combining these techniques with a strong work ethic, a positive attitude and sheer determination.

Dare to be a genius! Dare to read. Dare to develop intellect. Dare to work hard and show determination. Dare to think creatively. Dare to soar.

Clearly developing intellect is a key component of success. But so often we meet smart people who are not successful. We meet smart people who are not happy. We meet smart people who aren't likable. Being all that you can be is so much more than simply developing intellect. True success is built around feeding all the components that make us who we are.

What are those components? The Lakota Indians traditionally taught that each of us is like a small village made of four teepees: a mental, a physical, an emotional and a spiritual tent. They say "that while you can only live in one tent at a time, unless you go into every tent, every day, you are not complete." Traditional Chinese thought suggests that every person must maintain balance, and that if we want to feel truly open to life's opportunities we need to look carefully at our physical, mental, emotional and spiritual health. In Australia, the native aboriginal people believe that to remain healthy one must maintain a balance of physical, emotional, social, spiritual and intellectual health. In his ministry Oral Roberts proposed that God calls us to unity of body, mind and spirit. Psychologist and philosopher Abraham Maslow created a hierarchy of needs that suggests that there are four principal components of personhood: spiritual, mental, emotional and physical. To attain "self-actualization" you must first meet the underlying needs associated with these components.

I am not a disciple of Maslow or Roberts, nor do I suggest that you should adopt Native American customs or embrace eastern philosophy, but it does seem that each of these traditions has found a way to express a universal truth. To be complete we must find balance in our lives, and we must not neglect the intellectual, spiritual, emotional or physical aspects of our being.

Let's for a moment pretend that the below box represents your life:

If you were to divide this box to illustrate your life as you are living it today, how symmetrical would it be?

Mental	Emotional
Physical	Spiritual

Perhaps the reality today is that your life looks something like this:

Mental	Emotional
Physical	Spiritual

No matter how lopsided your life may be today, **dare to bring balance to your life.**

Mental	Emotional
Physical	Spiritual

Some people like to view this concept as

Mental
Emotional / Social
Physical
Religious / Spiritual

because they believe that a spiritual life is the foundation, the building block, of all that is important. This is probably true. But regardless of how you want to view these four essential aspects of your life, it is most important that you dedicate time to each one every day.

Dare to visit each tent every day. Dare to dedicate time to your mental, emotional, physical and spiritual life each and every day.

Chapter 4

Dare to Be Physically Strong

As a Scout you made a pledge to be physically strong. You said these words every time you uttered the Scout Oath. But what do they mean? Being strong is more than being able to lift heavy objects. Being physically strong means you can undertake physical activity without becoming tired or sore, and without getting out of breath. It means avoiding illness. As a young person these may seem like easy things to do. This is the most active time in your life. However unless you look at being physically strong differently, you are about to begin a slow downward spiral. Most people achieve their peak level of fitness between the ages of 18 and 21. Even if you are fit now, unless you change your lifestyle as you mature you are likely to not be fit 10 years from now. If you aren't currently physically strong, you have no time to waste. Now is the time to get started!

Why is it important to be physically strong? Think about people you know that are a success. Think about folks that you admire. When you put all the names that come into your mind together you will probably find that they are different in many ways. But I would imagine that most possess one trait in common: Energy. Nearly any successful person that you meet in life possesses a high energy level. How can you maintain a high energy level without health? How can you enthusiastically take on the challenges that await you in life if your body is not strong and you have no energy?

Nine Reasons to Exercise Daily:

1. Exercise improves your mood.
2. Exercise combats chronic disease.
3. Exercise helps you avoid colds.
4. Exercise boosts your brainpower.
5. Exercise helps you manage your weight.
6. Exercise boosts your energy level.
7. Exercise reduces stress.
8. Exercise promotes better sleep.
9. Exercise can be fun!

Health is the foundation for individual success. It is the foundation upon which all happiness depends. So many times I have seen men struggle through life working hard to finally reach a point where they are about to achieve success. But when they are at success's doorway, they have it snatched away from them because of physical failure. Don't pursue success at the cost of your body and your health. Keep physical fitness an important aspect of your life. It is easier to stay in shape than to try to make the arduous climb back to fitness if you have frittered away your health. There is no reason to let your health deteriorate in any way.

But exercise offers so many other benefits it's hard to understand why daily exercise is not an important part of everyone's life.

Exercise improves your mood. Physical activity stimulates various brain chemicals that will leave you feeling happier and more relaxed than you were before you started your workout. You'll also look better and feel better when you exercise regularly, which can boost your confidence and improve your self-esteem. Regular physical activity can even help prevent depression.

Exercise combats chronic disease. Regular exercise helps prevent heart disease, osteoporosis, diabetes, high blood pressure, high cholesterol and certain types of cancer. Exercise promotes development of strong bones and helps keep your bones strong. Exercising makes the heart and lungs stronger.

Exercise helps you avoid colds. Regular exercise appears to help jump-start the immune system, thus helping to reduce the number of colds, flu and other viruses.

Exercise boosts your brainpower. Exercise boosts blood flow to the brain and helps it receive oxygen and nutrients. The better shape you're in, the faster you fire brain waves that are responsible for quick thinking.

Exercise helps you manage your weight. As your metabolic rate improves, more calories are burned and you stay trimmer.

Exercise boosts your energy level. Physical activity delivers oxygen and nutrients to your tissues. Regular physical activity helps your cardiovascular system (the circulation of blood through your heart and blood vessels) work more efficiently. When your heart and lungs work more efficiently, you'll have more energy in everything you do.

Exercise reduces stress. It causes your body to release endorphins, or body chemicals that make you feel well.

Exercise promotes better sleep. Physical activity is often the key to better sleep. While we can fall asleep when we are mentally tired, becoming physically tired through physical activity can help you fall asleep faster and deepen your sleep. (Try not to exercise too close to bedtime; you may be too energized to fall asleep.) A good night's sleep can improve your concentration, productivity and mood.

Keeping fit is not a difficult job. It simply requires discipline and a little bit of time every day. While dedicating time to daily exercise is critically important, if you don't have time to exercise on a given day, make smart choices that will help you stay in shape. Take the stairs instead of the elevator. Walk during your lunch break. Park your car in a place that forces you to walk a little further. Dedicated workouts are the best way to go, but the physical activity you accumulate throughout the day helps you burn calories, too.

There is no great mystery about being physically strong — it is just common sense. It sounds so simple, yet it is a challenge few people meet. Too often, we don't exercise at all. We eat on the run. We don't get enough sleep. The result is a lack of energy that gives us an inability to exercise, get enough sleep and take the time needed to have healthy meals. Thus a vicious cycle begins.

Every day is a crucial test in the game of life. Every time you take liberties with your physical body, (not getting enough sleep, not eating right,) you are setting yourself up to pay a price later in life. You can't forever keep borrowing from your future. You need to carve a place for personal fitness into your life. You need to find a way to exercise every day.

Dare to be physically strong. Dare to eat right. Dare to exercise every day.

Chapter 5

Dare to Have Courage

As a scout you made a pledge to be brave. Bravery has always been a quality by which men measure themselves and others. What does it mean

> "The greatest test of courage on earth is to bear defeat without losing heart."
> – R. G. Ingersoll

to be brave? Bravery is not only showing the courage to face physical danger, but it involves having the determination to do what is right. This may mean standing up against those who are mean or critical of others. Courage is standing up for what you believe in without worrying about what other people might think. The real tests of courage come in everyday life, when we are faced with the choice of expedience versus doing what is right. Abandoning principles to go along with others is easy. Standing against cruelty, thoughtlessness and evil takes a deep, internal strength and personal risk. As a man of courage, you will be required to take difficult stands.

Courage can also be admitting that you're afraid and facing that fear directly. It's being strong enough to ask for help and humble enough to accept it. While most people consider bravery to be the ability to face bodily danger, more often the fears we face in life are not threats to our lives but rather are fears that exist in our minds. Often, true courage is related to overcoming a personal challenge rather than a true life and death struggle.

> "There is always danger for those who are afraid of it."
> - Dale Carnegie

Courage is following your own heart, living your own life, and settling for nothing less than the best for yourself. Courage is daring to take a first step, a big leap or a different path. It's attempting to do something that no one has done before, or that others thought impossible. Courage is being responsible for your own actions and admitting your mistakes without placing blame on others. It's relying not on others for your success, but on your own skills, abilities and efforts. Courage is setting a goal and refusing to quit, even when at times the goal may be seemingly impossible. Courage requires maintaining heart in the face of disappointment, and looking at defeat not as an end but as a new beginning. It's believing that things will ultimately get better even as they get worse. It's finding solutions to problems. It's not making excuses. Courage is thinking big, aiming high and shooting far. It's taking a dream and doing anything, risking everything and stopping at nothing to it make it a reality. The truth is, fear is the biggest obstacle that stands in the way of accomplishment.

Perhaps the biggest fear anyone faces in life is the fear to try something. What if we fail? More than anything else, fear of failure stops people from experiencing all that life can offer them. Fear of failure keeps most people from experiencing success. **Dare to try new things! Dare to take risks! Dare to fail!**

Yes, dare to fail. Many times we fail when we set out to accomplish a goal. But if we never even try, we are doomed to failure before we even start. NHL Star Wayne Gretsky once said, "You miss 100% of the

> You have to try
> "You miss 100% of the shots you never take."
> - Wayne Gretsky, NHL All-Star

shots you never take." He's right. In order to score you need to shoot the puck. To hit a home run you need to swing the bat. Many people spend their entire lives with the bat sitting on their shoulders. **Dare to swing the bat! There is a chance you may strike out. But there is also a chance for you to hit a home run!**

And what if your strike out? Your life will forever change the day you realize that it's ok to strike out. Even the best major league hitters fail about 70% of the time. But that's no reason for them to stop playing baseball. If getting a hit were easy, it wouldn't be fun. The more difficult the challenge, the more spectacular the victory. What we obtain too easily we regard too lightly. Nothing worth having in life comes without the price of challenge and hard work. And despite hard work and great effort, we don't always win.

> "Life shrinks or expands in proportion to one's courage."
> - Anais Nin

If everything always turned out just the way you wanted it to, your life would be a boring repetition of stale successes. In failure we are challenged. We need to find the strength to get up and try again. Be a man that can smile in the face of trouble, who gathers strength from tribulations, and grows brave as a result of facing obstacles. If you can respond to failure in this way, you will be a winner in the marathon of life. Those who have never failed will never fully taste the sweetness of victory.

If you are willing to go out and try to do things; if you are willing to risk failure, your life will be much more fulfilling. Your life will shrink or expand in proportion to your courage. If you want to conquer fear don't sit home dwelling on it. Go out, get busy, become a man of action. **Dare to do things!**

Courage is not in fact the absence of fear, but it is instead the ability to carry on in spite of it. If you are afraid of heights, it's time to go climb a hill, so that tomorrow you are ready to take on a mountain. If you are afraid to talk in public, go out and force yourself to speak in front of a group. Like a muscle, courage is strengthened by use. Facing small fears each and every day makes us strong enough to face big challenges when they arise. Ironically, fear, when properly channeled and controlled, can breed creativity, strength and objectivity. A Scout is brave not by ridding himself of fear, but by manipulating fear to his own advantage. Don't ever let yourself surrender to fear! Learn to control it. If you learn how to make fear work for you, it will become one of your best friends.

Fear is not the only obstacle that stops us from attaining our goals. We can delude ourselves into waiting to go after our goals until some obstacle is out of our way. We say to ourselves, I'll learn to play guitar after I graduate from high school. Or, I'll find a new job after I pay off my student loans. Don't wait! **Dare to be a man of action!**

I often ask my Scouts this simple question. If there are 10 frogs on a log, and nine decide to jump, how many are left? The answer is ten. Because there is a big difference between deciding and doing. When we decide to do something tomorrow, we are really deciding not to do something at all. A Scout is action-oriented. He gets things done. Don't wait until tomorrow; do what you can do today.

Every year when new Scouts join our troop, we introduce them to Scouting with this little exercise. I have our existing Scouts line up chairs creating an obstacle course. I then ask each of the new Scouts to take a moment and to study the pattern of chairs. Then we blindfold each of the new Scouts and ask them to traverse the obstacle course.

As soon as each of the Scouts is blindfolded we quietly remove all the chairs and then we watch as each Scout gingerly wanders across the room trying to avoid the obstacles.

Life is like this game. We spend our lives avoiding obstacles we have created for ourselves, and in reality exist only in our minds. We're afraid to take piano lessons, try out for the school play, learn a foreign language, contact an old friend – whatever we would really like to do but don't because of perceived obstacles. Don't avoid the "chairs" that exist in your life until you smack into one. And if you do at least you'll have a place to sit down.

Toward the end of World War II, the guards at a Japanese concentration camp learned that the American troops were just days away from overrunning their compound. Late in the evening, when the prisoners were asleep, the guards unlocked all the gates and fled into the woods. For the next two days, the prisoners remained within the prison walls, without food or water. Finally, when American Troops reached the compound, they only needed to announce to the prisoners that they were already free.

We too can be like these prisoners of war. In our minds are obstacles, prison walls, which keep us from being happy. By accepting the prison walls around us, we place limits on ourselves, and on what we can become. If you want to find true happiness and to reach your potential, you need to test the gates every day.

Perhaps the obstacle that stops you from pursuing your dream is that you lack a particular ability. Scott Adams, the creator of Dilbert, couldn't draw very well. He took his first cartooning class at the age of 40. If you go back and look at the drawings in his first books you'll see his cartooning skills were quite limited. Yet he went on to become the highest grossing cartoonist in the industry. He did this not through innate ability. He was a success simply because he showed determination and he wasn't afraid to try.

I have a great deal of respect for the music group the Wiggles. You're probably wondering why. We all know many better musicians. Truth be told, the

Wiggles are not great singers. They can't dance. The songs they craft won't be top 10 singles. So what is it about the Wiggles that I like? I have respect for the Wiggles because of their shortcomings. There are literally thousands of people with more talent, yet these four men had the audacity to try to do what they loved. They had the conviction of an idea and rose to the top through hard work and creativity. They rose to the top because they had the courage to try. **Dare to try**. **Dare to do things you enjoy! Dare to follow your dreams! Dare to pursue your goals!**

Astronaut Alan Beam was once asked what he thought was the most important trait a successful person has. He answered by saying, "Successful people have a dream. They think and work toward that goal every day." What did you do today to move you closer to your dream? Don't put off taking action. The journey of a thousand miles starts with the first step. **Dare to take a step!**

The best way to predict the future is to create it. If opportunity doesn't knock, **Dare to build a door! Dare to create your future** rather than simply letting life happen!

As an Eagle Scout you have already taken a step toward creating your future. You have accomplished a significant goal. Did you set this goal? Did you make a decision to become an Eagle Scout, or was this a goal set for you by someone else, perhaps your friends, your parents or your Scoutmaster? You are now at an age where you need to live your own life. You need to set your own goals. If you want to accomplish anything meaningful the first step to accomplishment is deciding exactly what it is you want to do. Goal setting is a powerful process for envisioning your ideal future and motivating yourself to turn this vision of the future into reality.

The process of setting goals helps you choose where you want to go. Rather than sitting back and letting life happen, by setting goals you can take control of your life and steer yourself to exactly where you want to go. By knowing what you want to achieve, you will know what steps you need to take to help you arrive at your destination. You'll also easily spot distractions that would otherwise divert you from your course.

Most people drift through life following whatever path they happen to stumble upon. They have no idea where this path will lead them. If you don't know where you are going, any path will do. You need to decide where you are going so that you can choose the path that will lead you there.

For many young people, this is a hard thing to do. Maybe you don't know exactly what you want out of life. Maybe you don't know what to pursue for a career. It's okay not to have your entire life mapped out before you're even 18 years old. But you should still take some time to consider what your goals are right now. Writing these goals down will help you begin to develop a direction. As you mature and gain more insight, you can refine these goals. When you put your list of goals together, be sure to include something related to education. Learning about a broad variety of subjects is a worthwhile goal for everyone. Pursuing a broad liberal arts-based education can help you learn about a wide variety of topics, and can help you discover your true calling in life.

Starting to Set Goals

When you create your initial list of goals, try and set goals on a number of different levels. First, try to establish lifetime goals related to what you want to do with your life. Then, break these goals down into smaller goals that you must hit along the way in order to reach your lifetime goals. When establishing your lifetime goals, don't think only about financial and career goals, but try to set goals related to all important aspects of your life, including the following categories:

Education
Is there a knowledge area you need to bolster to accomplish your life goals?
What information and skills will you need to achieve your career goals?
What information and skills will you need to achieve your other personal goals?

Family
Do you want to get married?
Do you want to be a parent?
If so, what do you need to do now to position yourself to find the right partner and to be a good parent?

Physical
Do you wish to live a long and healthy life?
What steps are you going to take to achieve this?

Spiritual

Do you want to have a close relationship with God?
What things do you need to do to improve your spiritual life?
What things do you need to stop doing?
What do you need to read, hear or learn in order to better understand your faith?

Attitude

Is there any aspect of your attitude that is holding you back?
Do you need to learn to think more positively?
Are you afraid to try things?
Is there any part of the way that you behave that upsets you?
If the answer to any of these questions is yes, set goals to help you improve your attitude. This is one of the most important goals you can set.

Creative

Do you want to achieve any creative goals?
Do you want to accomplish anything related to music, art or journalism?
Do you have interest in writing a book?
What do you need to do now to position yourself to pursue these goals?

Spend some time brainstorming in these areas, and then select a small number of significant goals in each category that you can focus on. When you do this, make sure that the goals that you set are ones that you genuinely want to achieve, not ones that your parents, Scout leaders or friends might want for you. Remain true to yourself.

Achieve Your Lifetime Goals
Once you have set your lifetime goals, develop shorter-term goals that you will need to complete if you wish to reach your lifetime goals. Turn these shorter-term goals into an action list of daily and weekly tasks you will need to complete in order to accomplish these shorter term goals.

Goal Setting Tips
Try to keep the following thoughts in mind in order to set the most effective goals:

1. State each goal as a positive statement: "Graduate from high school" is a positive goal, stating the goal as "don't flunk out" would be a negative statement.

2. Be precise: Set specific goals that include amounts or dates that could be used to help measure success.

3. Set priorities: Determine which goals are most important so that when you have to make a decision to do one thing versus another you can make better choices.

4. Commit your goals to paper: Writing down goals crystallizes the goal and puts the force of your words behind them.

5. Make short-term goals small enough to be achievable. It's much easier to accomplish a series of small goals than to accomplish a large goal. Setting short term goals and achieving them creates a feeling of accomplishment that can help spur you on to completing longer-term goals.

Properly-set goals can be an incredibly motivating force in your life. As you get into the habit of setting and achieving goals, you'll build self-confidence. This will induce you to set and achieve more goals. Goal setting can help you organize your time and resources to help you get the most out of your life. You can see forward progress in daily tasks that might otherwise have felt like a pointless grind. **Dare to set goals for yourself! Dare to accomplish these goals! Dare to not be afraid to try!**

Positive Affirmations

Once you have established your goals, consider using Positive Affirmations as a tool to help keep you on track. What are Positive Affirmations? Positive Affirmations are statements that describe a desired situation or goal. They are statements that can be repeated, until they are implanted and embraced by the subconscious mind. The process of making affirmations causes the subconscious mind to strive and work on your behalf to make these positive statements come true.

Positive Affirmations work. They are a very powerful tool that can aid you on your journey toward success. When you use this method properly, affirmations will help you improve your life.

I did not know anything about positive affirmations early in my life. However, in my efforts to not take myself too seriously, whenever I did something dumb I would remind myself that I was a genius. And the dumber the things I did, the more of a super genius I would tell myself I was. And quite by accident, I began a process of making positive affirmations an ongoing part of my life. I didn't know I was using positive affirmations, and I didn't understand the science of why these affirmations worked. I simply knew that this approach to handling negative events was having a beneficial effect on me. My mind started finding creative ways to overcome obstacles.

When I discovered positive affirmations were a formal process, I began to understand the science behind why this method worked. When you master using affirmations, you'll have a valuable tool for improving your life.

Most people have a tendency to focus on the negative. They repeat in their minds negative words and statements concerning their life circumstances and events. These words reinforce negativity; they are effectively negative affirmations that start a process of creating a pessimistic outlook. These words and thoughts lead the subconscious mind to the conclusion that a goal can't be reached, and therefore the subconscious mind stops trying.

Words work both ways, and it is the process of countering this gloomy thought process with bright encouraging statements that turns a harmful thought process into a beneficial one. This is because your subconscious mind accepts statements as true if you keep saying them. Your mind attracts corresponding events and situations into your life. So why not choose only positive statements, in order to get positive results?

Imagine that you are jogging with your friends. They plan to run two miles, something you have never done before. You want to hang with your friends so you start running, and while you run, you keep repeating in your mind, "I can do this, I can do this." You keep thinking and believing that you can run for two miles. You are repeating positive affirmations.

Now imagine you had said to yourself, "I cannot do this", "I'll never make it", "It's too far." These kinds of statements would cause you to lose ambition, confidence and motivation, and would lead to the negative result that you had predicted.

Consider the thoughts that run through your mind and the words that you use every day. Do you ever find yourself saying things like:

"I cannot do this."
"This project is too much for me."
"I'm never going to get this job."
"This is not going to work out."
"I lack inner strength."
"I am going to fail."
"This can't be done."
"It's too much work."

These negative words and thoughts program the mind to produce negative results much like you might program a computer. Conversely, repeating positive statements will help you focus your mind on taking actions toward accomplishing your goals. Positive statements also create corresponding mental images in the conscious mind that affect the subconscious mind accordingly. In this way, you program your subconscious in accordance with your will. Your subconscious mind starts to visualize your goals and works creatively to formulate pathways that will lead you to them. The conscious mind, the mind you think with, starts this process, and later the subconscious mind takes charge.

By using the process of positive affirmations consciously and intently, you influence your subconscious mind. In turn, your mind transforms your habits, behavior, attitude and reactions, and reshapes your external life.

You might wonder, can this really work? How long might it take to get results? Sometimes the effect of this process can be seen almost immediately. This depends on your focus, faith, strength of desire, and the feelings you put into the words, and on how big or small is your goal is. It is important to understand that repeating positive affirmations for a few minutes will only be effective if you proceed to avoid negative thinking through the day. If you make affirmations and then think negatively, your negative thoughts will neutralize the effects of the positive ones. If you want to get positive results you have to refuse to think negatively.

How do you go about making Positive Affirmations?

1. Focus on your thoughts.
2. Repeat them every time your mind is not engaged in something important.
3. Say them if you experience something that leads you away from your goal to counteract that negative experience.
4. Be as relaxed as you can when you make your affirmations.
5. Pay full attention to the words you are repeating.
6. Say these words slowly.
7. Put your faith into what you are saying.

Follow the 4 rules of making positive affirmations.

1. Choose affirmations that are not too long.

2. Choose affirmations that are specific.

3. State your affirmations in a positive way. Don't use negative words or words with negative connotations in your affirmations. For example, if your goal is weight loss, don't say, "I am getting less fat." Instead say, "I am getting slimmer every day." Plant positive mental images in your mind.

4. State your affirmations in the present tense. For example, saying "I will be wealthy" means that you intend to be rich one day, in the indefinite future, but not now. It is more effective to say, and "I am wealthy" and try to embrace the feeling of wealth as you say this. The subconscious mind will work overtime to make this happen now, in the present. By stating what you want to be true in your life, you mentally and emotionally see and feel it as true, irrespective of your current circumstances, and thereby attract it into your life.

Affirmations.

Affirmations are words with power.

Affirmations channel the work of your subconscious mind.

Affirmations make you feel happy.

Affirmations allow you to focus on your goals.

Some examples of Positive Affirmations:
I am a good student.
I have a lot of energy.
I am getting wealthier every day.
I feel great.
I get better looking every day.
I am slimmer.
Wealth is pouring into my life.
My mind is calm.
I am good at math.
I don't get angry.
I can learn this material quickly.
I am blessed.
I am beautiful.
I am worthy.
I have loving, positive and happy thoughts.
I am happy.
I am healthy.
I am wealthy.
I am secure.
I am positive.
I am smart.
I am creative.
I am self-reliant.
I am a problem solver.
I know how to get things done.
I find solutions.
I am blessed.
I am grateful for all the goodness in my life.
A positive relationship is entering my life.
I am energetic and enthusiastic.
I always see the good in others and myself.
I am outgoing.

I love change and I adjust easily to new situations.
I have good and loving relations.
I am calm and relaxed in every situation.
I never feel angry.
I have everything that I need in my life.
I can laugh and feel happy no matter what happens.
I am bringing beneficial changes into my life.
I bring my best to every situation.
Good things are happening in my life.
I am sailing on the river of wealth.
I study and comprehend quickly.
My thoughts are under my control.
I have the means to travel whenever I want to.
I am courageous.
I radiate love and happiness.
I am well liked.
I am gifted.
I am an amazing person.
People want to be like me.
I am talented.
I am totally at peace.
My body is getting leaner, lighter, fitter and tighter.
I turn challenges into opportunities.
I am surrounded by love.
I have the perfect job for me.
I am kind.
I am happy about where I am living.
I have a wonderful and satisfying job.
I am a good person.
I have an unending desire to be a better person and
to make myself a better person.
I enjoy being alone.
I have a bright future.

I am open to all possibilities.
I have purpose and direction.
I use my time alone to bring focus to my life.
I save money easily, there is nothing I really need to buy.
I have forgiven myself for the past.
I trust myself.
I make the right choices every time.
I matter and what I have to offer this world also matters.
I trust my wisdom and intuition.
This situation is working out for my best.
Good things unfold before me.
I am understanding and compassionate.
I will find the good in this situation.
I muster hope and courage from deep inside me.
I find hopeful and optimistic ways to look at things.
I know my wisdom guides me to the right decision.
I trust myself to make the best decision for me.
I will make the decision that is best for me.
I love my family even if they do not understand me completely.
I see my family as a gift.
I am a better person because I go through hardship.
I am smart and interesting and that's how everyone sees me.
I never know what amazing incredible person I will meet next.
The company of strangers teaches me more about my own likes and dislikes.
I am doing work that I enjoy and find fulfilling.
What I do matters and I play a role in helping others.
I find ways to follow my dreams.
I never get defensive.

Some of the most powerful affirmations you can make include:

I have a deep inner strength.
Setbacks are temporary and only make me stronger and more determined.
I love the person I have become.
I am a genius.
I never give up; I find ways to reach my destination.
I am doing things that make me a success.

Affirmations can also be used to help you face specific issues:

When you can't sleep
Peaceful sleep awaits me in dreamland.
I embrace the peace and quiet of the night.

When you don't want to face the day
This day brings me nothing but joy.
I make every day special.
I am feeling better every day.
Each day, I do things that lead me toward my goal.
I am excited about today.
Everything is getting better every day.

When you worry about your future
I make smart, calculated plans for my future.
I am a money magnet and I attract wealth and abundance.
I am in complete charge of my future.
I trust in my own ability to provide well for my family.

When you come face to face with a problem
Everything works out for my highest good.
There is a great reason this is unfolding before me now.
I'll find a new way of thinking about this situation.

When you need confidence
I see myself as a gift to my people and community and nation.
I am a good person and I do good things.
Confidence is my nature.
I am good at _____.
I believe in myself and my abilities.
I am successful in whatever I do.

When overcoming illness
My body is healing.
My body is healthy and functioning in a very good way.

When feeling lonely
Being alone makes me feel happy and gives me time to think.
I feel the love of those who are not physically around me.

The kinds of affirmations you can make are limitless. As positive affirmations have become more and more popular, the Web is becoming littered with lists of affirmations. Unfortunately, many of these lists contain "affirmations" that are not really positive affirmations. Instead, these lists are made up of feel good expressions or coping phrases for dealing with problems, rather than being positive, present focus statements to help focus your subconscious mind.

Here are some examples of affirmations you might find on the Web that violate one of the 4 important rules of Positive Affirmations:

"I choose to find hopeful and optimistic ways to look at this."
Wrong: This is incorrect, it violates rule 3. The affirmation is not stated as a positive. Don't use "choose" in an affirmation. Don't "choose", instead "do."
Here is a positive way to restate that affirmation:
"I find optimistic ways to look at this."

I let go of worries that drain my energy.
Wrong: This violates rule 3, it contains a negative statement. Instead say:
"I don't worry about the future."

It's too early to give up on my goals.
Wrong, violates rule 3 it's a negative statement. Instead say:
"I will reach my goals."

I replace my anger with understanding and compassion.
Wrong, rule 3. Instead say:
"I am understanding and compassionate."

I listen lovingly to this inner conflict and reflect on it until I get to peace around it.
Wrong violates rule 1, its too long, instead say:
"I will make the right decision."

Hopefully this gives you the insight to formulate your own positive affirmations. Used properly Positive Affirmations are a powerful tool, but used improperly, as many are starting to use them today, they won't have much benefit. So when employing affirmations, be sure to understand what Positive Affirmations truly are and state your affirmations in a way that channels your subconscious mind to work on your behalf.

Chapter 6

Dare to Be a Man of Character

You may think this sounds easy. You may think that you already are a person of character. But what really is character? And how can you develop character? Character is a set of behavioral traits that define who you are. You demonstrate character by doing what is right. But what is right? To have character you must first have beliefs. Character is, simply put, developing a strong sense of right and wrong and living your life in accordance with this sense.

> **Character**
>
> "The measure of a man's real character is what he would do if he knew he would never be found out."
>
> – Thomas Macaulay

Character is different from almost any other trait. It is the only thing in the world not for sale. True character knows no price. It is expressed in the way a man acts regardless of the potential financial reward. It is equally abandoned by the theft of ten dollars or ten cents.

Character cannot be developed in ease and quiet. Only through trials and suffering can the soul be strengthened. Remaining principled in the long term requires short-term difficulties. These difficulties are a testing ground. If you have the character to endure small trials, perhaps you will pass the test of greater ones. If you do not have what it takes to endure small trials, you certainly won't endure greater ones. Character is not built in times of emergency; it is simply exhibited. Character cannot be summoned at the moment of crisis if it has been squandered by years of compromise and rationalization. The only testing ground for the heroic is the mundane. The only preparation for that one profound decision which can change a life, or even a nation, is those hundreds of half-conscious, self-defining, seemingly insignificant decisions made in private. Habit is the daily battleground of character.

You may be concerned about having people like you. You may want to have a good reputation. Be more concerned with your character than with being liked. Be more concerned with your character than your reputation. Your character is who you really are, while your reputation is merely what others think of you. Be more concerned with your character than with success. Success is always temporary. When all is said and done, all you have left is character. **Dare to be a person of great character.**

> **Effort**
> "The healthiest competition occurs when average people win by putting in above average effort."
> - Colin Powell

It is hard to talk about character without thinking about faith. Have you met a man of great character who did not have a relationship with God? A Scout is reverent and believes in God. Developing a close relationship with God and developing character go hand-in-hand. If you don't currently have a relationship with God you need to. If you have a relationship with God you need to keep that relationship in a place of prominence in your life. Building a relationship with God will cause you to grow. It will place you on a higher level and allow you to focus on things beyond yourself. A relationship with God will allow you to lift your thoughts above the commonplace, and focus on what's noble.

Developing a strong spiritual foundation will also help you in your decision-making. You have thousands of decisions ahead of you, and even the smallest decision can affect whether or not you get to where you are trying to go. Faith will allow you to try to go to places where you would not otherwise dare to go— to look beyond what appears probable and to try to do the improbable. Faith allows you to look reality in the face and deny it. To ignore the odds and to set out to do the impossible. Faith is knowing that with man some things are impossible but with God all things are possible. There is no limit to what you can accomplish with God by your side.

Perhaps there is no better example of a life of faith than mother Theresa of Calcutta. Relying on nothing other than faith, this 4'10" inch women rose from obscurity to win the Nobel peace prize for her service to the poor, which included establishing 517 missions in more than 100 countries. At one such mission in Calcutta, her nuns provided "breadcakes" to the poor for lunch each day. The story is told that one morning one of the novices who worked in the kitchen came up to Mother Theresa and said, "We have no flour to bake bread for lunch. We have planned poorly." The situation looked bleak, as there were more than 300 mouths to feed in less than two hours' time, and there was no food. The novice expected Mother Theresa to phone some of her benefactors in an effort to muster up enough money to buy some food. Instead, Mother Theresa's spontaneous reaction was to say to the novice, "Sister, you are in charge of the kitchen this week. Go into the chapel and tell Jesus we have no food. That's settled, now let's move on. What's next?"

Mother Theresa did not give the matter another thought until about 10 minutes later when there was a knock at the door. Mother Theresa was called down. A man whom she had never seen before addressed her saying, "we were just informed that the teachers at the city schools are going on strike. Classes have been dismissed and we have 5,000 lunches that we don't know what to do with. Can you help us use them?"

Mother Theresa lived a life accomplishing great things because of her faith. Few will ever possess her level of faith but without some level of faith it is difficult to accomplish anything. Miracles happen only to those who believe in them. Your vision of what can be accomplished is directly proportional to the amount of your faith. The world's greatest feats have been accomplished by people with too much faith to know they were impossible. **Dare to be a man of faith!**

Faith is an important component of character. If you want to lead others you must have character and faith. All great leaders have character. As General H. Norman Schwarzkopf once said, leadership is a potent combination of strategy and character. But if you must be without one, be without the strategy. To say that you can have leadership without character would be like saying that there can be sunshine without light. To say that you can have leadership without faith is like saying you can have snow without cold. Character and faith keep leaders driving unceasingly toward their goal. With faith, leaders overcome great challenges. Leadership is all about seeing the world as it should be and changing it through character, faith and effort. **Dare to be a man of character. Dare to walk the straight line.**

What does walking the straight line mean? Late in life, George Washington was asked by a close friend for an explanation of how he enjoyed such remarkable success. How did Washington lead America to a seemingly impossible victory against the British in the Revolutionary War?

George Washington had an interesting and unusual reply. He said, "I always walked a straight line." As a youth, he acquired a positive love of the right and he developed an iron will to do what is right. With Washington, what you saw was what you got; the public man and the private man were one and the same.

Washington earned the loyalty of the men who served with him not because of personal charisma or oratorical skills but because of his reliable integrity, incorruptible judgment and persevering zeal. What he was, he made himself by will, effort, self-discipline, ambition and perseverance. George Washington had the strength he needed for the long and dangerous journeys of his incredible life because he always walked the "straight line." Prepare yourself for life's journey by walking that same straight line.

Just as George Washington served his Country, as an Eagle Scout you are called upon to do your duty to God and your Country. You may not have the same opportunity as Washington to help forge a new nation based on the principles of life, liberty and the pursuit of happiness. Still, as Americans, we all have a responsibility to keep our Country safe and secure and to do our part to help America remain the greatest Country on earth. Joining the military can be a great way to serve your Country, but if military service is not your calling, it does not relinquish you from a responsibility to serve. But if you don't join the military how can you serve?

Defending freedom is one of the most important ways that all Americans can serve their Country. Everyone wants to live in freedom, yet many people forget that living in a free

> We bring glory to God by serving others.

society carries with it certain obligations. You must honor the rights of others. You must respect the law and you must defend the rights of others to exercise their freedoms, even when you don't agree with them. You must embrace these principles as if the future of America depends upon it. Because it does. If Americans stopped protecting these duties and obligations, our Country as we know it would cease to exist. It is the citizen's acceptance of these responsibilities that keeps America free.

President John F. Kennedy once said, "Ask not what your Country can do for you but ask what you can do for your Country." That's quite a challenge. It's easy to sit back and expect those in government to be the ones to do everything, but the truth is it is the duty of every citizen to create the nation or change that they would like to see. Most things that can be done to serve the nation are very simple but they require the collective efforts of hundreds of people doing little things every day. Here are some things you can do as part of your everyday life to serve your nation:

1. Contact your local political representatives about key issues.
2. Write a letter to the editor about an issue you care about.
3. Offer to pass out election materials.
4. Register people to vote.
5. Vote.
6. Organize a public issues forum for your neighborhood.
7. Volunteer at a polling booth on the day of an election.
8. Volunteer to shuttle those that need rides to the polls on Election Day.
9. Read books or the newspaper on tape for visually impaired people.
10. Visit, entertain or bring toys to children in the cancer ward of a hospital.
11. Help teach a younger child to read.
12. Volunteer at a homeless shelter.
13. Organize a canned goods drive.
14. Gather clothing from your neighbors and donate it to a local shelter.

15. Collect supplies like combs, toothbrushes, shampoo, etc. for the homeless.
16. Deliver meals to homebound individuals.
17. Make quilts or baby clothes for low-income families.
18. Get together with friends to buy Christmas presents for a family at a shelter.
19. Offer opportunity to those less fortunate.
20. Teach Sunday school.
21. Coach a youth sports team.
22. Become a Scout leader.
23. Mentor young people and train the next generation of Americans.
24. Paint a mural over graffiti.
25. Tutor someone that needs help learning English or some other subject.
26. Plant flowers in public areas that could benefit from some color.
27. Plant a garden or tree where the whole neighborhood can enjoy it.
28. Clean up a vacant lot or park.
29. Organize a campaign to raise money to purchase and install playground equipment.
30. Clean up trash along a river, on a beach or in a park.
31. Volunteer to help at a Special Olympics event.
32. Send a letter or package to an American veteran or overseas soldier.
33. Donate books to your local library.
34. Donate an old computer to a school.
35. Become an organ donor.
36. Do business ethically.
37. Pay your taxes in full and on time.

38. Learn first aid.
39. Become CPR certified.
40. Give blood.
41. Shop at local, family owned businesses.
42. Become a big brother or big sister.
43. Write a note to thank a volunteer or teacher that had a positive effect on your life.
44. Recycle.
45. Volunteer at a crisis pregnancy center.
46. Drive responsibly.
47. Dispose of litter appropriately.
48. Shop responsibly.
49. Support an adoption.
50. Teach at an adult literacy center.
51. Coordinate a book drive.
52. Donate money to your favorite charity.
53. Buy American.
54. Reduce your energy consumption.
55. Donate toys or suitcases to foster children.
56. When visiting someone in a hospital, talk to someone that doesn't have many visitors.
57. Pay your debts.
58. Run your business with integrity.
59. Serve on a jury.
60. Run for an elected office.
61. Become a civil servant.
62. Serve on a school board, zoning board, or city or town commission.
63. Join AmeriCorps.
64. Join the Peace Corp.

Dare to take on some of the above challenges. Dare to become someone that helps make our Country work. Dare to serve your Country.

In the Scout Oath we make a pledge to do our duty to God and our Country. How do we go about serving God? In many cases, our Duty to God and Duty to our Country can require doing the same thing. As people of faith and American citizens we are called to give service to others. While people of faith can view the question of duty to God differently, in many a duty to God can include:

1. Help those in need. (Benevolence)
2. Assist others when they cannot assist themselves. (Paternalism)
3. Do not harm others.
4. Do not deceive others. (Honesty)
5. Obey God's laws. (Lawfulness)
6. Respect freedom of others. (Autonomy)
7. Respect the life of others.
8. Honor God. (Reverence)
9. Prayer, worship and contemplation.
10. Give praise and thanks.

In what ways can you take action to fulfill your Duty to God? Here are some ideas:

1. Share faith with others.
Bring people closer to God by sharing your faith with others. As we give of ourselves in the service of God and others, we will be greatly blessed.

2. Serve God through your family.
Service to God starts with service to your family. Support the needs of your parents, children brothers and sisters.

3. Volunteer in your community.

There are countless ways to serve God by serving in your community. Many volunteer opportunities are mentioned earlier in the section on 60 ways to serve your Country.

4. Serve God by serving children.

So many children and teenagers are in need of love and support. You can be a youth leader, Scout leader, mentor or big brother who provides that support.

5. Donate clothing and other goods.

Generously give those things that you are not using to those in need.

6. Be a friend.

One of the simplest and easiest ways to serve God and others is by befriending one another.

7. Share your talents.

Use your God given abilities to help others improve their lives. This can have a greater impact than bringing them food or clothing

8. Mourn with those who mourn.

Support someone who has lost a loved one.

9. Follow God's inspiration.

Open your heart and your mind to God's inspiration. If your heart tells you to do something positive to help others, follow that inspiration.

10. Support your church and other charities financially.

One of the ways we can serve God is by helping his children, our brothers and sisters who are in need by providing them with financial support.

11. Perform simple acts of service.

To serve God we must do little things to help others each and every day.

12. Be open to God's calling you to a life of service.

Perhaps God is calling you to a life dedicated to your faith. Be open to God's calling. Become a Priest, Minister or Missionary. Take an active role as a lay person in your church, temple or synagogue.

13. Be an example of God's love by the way you live your life.

Every day we are given opportunities to smile, be friendly, hold open a door or help someone. Be an example of God's love by seizing these opportunities to bring small joys to those your encounter. Sometimes the best chances to serve God are presented in the way we interact with others.

14. Regularly attend a place of Worship.

I often hear Scouts ask, "Do we really need to spend time in a temple, church or synagogue every week to be reverent?" Or, "Can we simply worship God as we ride our bicycles or play at the park?" While we can worship God anywhere, the truth is, worship is scarcely as frequent in those places as in houses built in His honor. There is the story of the father who said, "Come on, we can sing hymns on the beach," to which his son replied, "But we won't, will we." There is a time and place for everything; and fulfilling our Duty to God requires keeping a time and place for God in our lives. **Dare to do your Duty to God!** As Scouts we are presented with many other challenges related to character. The law dares Scouts to be trustworthy, loyal, obedient and reverent. In the Oath you are challenged to be morally straight. What does it mean to be morally straight? In simple terms, we are called to know what is right and true, to love what is good, and to choose to do what is right at every opportunity. Just as you need to exercise frequently to be physically strong, to be morally straight you need to make choices every day that are in line with your values and beliefs. You can be honest and you can help others. You can think about the needs of others. You can respect your body and you can be respectful of others. You can act in a manner that leaves the world a little better for your having been there.

The exercise of building moral strength is simply doing little things every day in keeping with your beliefs and conscience. Before you can be morally straight when it comes to life's big challenges, you need to first exercise your spirit. You do this by keeping morally straight when given the opportunity each and every day.

Dare to be morally straight. Dare to do what is right each and every day. Dare to show good character by being trustworthy, loyal, obedient and reverent. Dare to be a man of faith. Dare to be a man of character.

Chapter 7

Dare to Have Charisma

I consider the attainment of the Eagle Scout rank one of the great honors and accomplishments that a young man can achieve. I am pre-disposed to think highly of Eagle Scouts. I believe they possess something that others lack. This includes a certain drive and determination. A quiet kind of confidence that comes from completing the trail of discovery that one walks on his way to becoming an Eagle Scout.

Very recently, I reviewed a resume from a young Eagle Scout who had just graduated from college. He had an outstanding looking resume and excellent grades. On paper he was undoubtedly the most qualified candidate I would be interviewing for one of our entry-level job openings. However when this candidate came in for his job interview I was most unimpressed. Yes, he had outstanding academic credentials and was probably quite smart, but he demonstrated no personality. In the interview he was not especially likable or dynamic. There was in fact nothing compelling about his personality. He had no charisma. Having a personality that draws others to you and being likable, are among the most important traits needed to find success in life, regardless of your chosen path or profession. The truly successful, the top 1% in any field, are more likely to have a charismatic personality than they are to be among the most intelligent in their field. **Dare to have Charisma! Dare to develop a personality that makes people want to be around you!**

You may feel you are shy by nature. You may feel your personality is something you are born with, and it is not something that can be changed. While there are many character traits that are natural for us, it wrong to suggest that it is natural for someone not to be likable. Quiet people can be likable. Loud people can be likable. Likable people can be short or tall, black or white. There is nothing innate about us as people that makes us likable or unlikable. What makes us this way is the way we behave.

A Scout is friendly, courteous, kind, obedient and cheerful. These are traits that one must exhibit to be liked. Did you somehow become an Eagle Scout without developing these traits? Having charisma is all about putting others before yourself. It is behaving in a way that is thoughtful of others. It is acting in a way that makes other people feel comfortable.

Recently, I went to an event where five boys from different schools were brought together to work on a project. Each boy that

> A Scout is friendly.

entered the room knew none of the others. Each admittedly felt slightly out of place and uncomfortable. But one boy, I'll call him Robert, walked in and introduced himself to each of the others. Robert tried to make the other boys feel comfortable, and he asked each one a little something about themselves. Soon, a moderator called the youths together and asked them to begin their project by selecting a group leader. The boys unanimously selected Robert. Was Robert more qualified? No one really knew. Was Robert better looking, taller, thinner, stronger or smarter than the others? Undoubtedly he was not. So why was Robert selected? Despite the fact that Robert was as nervous and uncomfortable as all the others, Robert did his best to think about the other boys and to try and make them feel comfortable. In his concern, he came across as being caring and confident. These are traits people want in a leader.

I know another young man who completely lacked confidence. He was so afraid that people would realize how lacking his confidence was that he began pretending he was confident. Anyone who knows him today will tell you he is the most confident person they have ever met. Confidence is not just about how you feel, it's about the way that you are perceived. **Dare to be confident**. And if you don't have confidence, **Dare to pretend to be confident.** No one will know the difference.

Professional tennis player Arthur Ashe believed that "the key to self-confidence is preparation." **Dare to Be Prepared**. It is much easier to have self-confidence when you know what you are doing. When you are trained to handle what comes at you in life, when you have practiced and are physically fit it is hard not to feel some level of confidence. So **Dare to Be Prepared**. Do little things every day to be mentally and physically fit to face any situation.

Preparation gives rise to confidence and confidence breeds Charisma.

In the race of life, if you have no confidence in yourself, you are defeated before you start. With confidence, you have won even before you have started.

It is important however, not to confuse confidence with arrogance. An arrogant person acts superior to others. Arrogance implies acting in a condescending way and showing a lack of courtesy and grace. Confidence is, in a sense, the complete opposite of arrogance. An arrogant person belittles others and makes them feel ill at ease. A confident person goes outside of themselves to make others feel welcome and relaxed.

Have you ever met someone who is always ready to complain? They are always sick, tired or overworked and are always anxious to tell you about it? How excited are you to talk to someone like that? The truth is that no one wants to be surrounded by misery but everyone wants to spend time with someone who is positive and uplifting. If you want to have Charisma, you need to be positive in your interactions with others.

Andre Maurois once said, "Smile, for everyone lacks self-confidence and more than any other one thing a smile reassures them." This is a statement I have found to be so very true. It doesn't cost anything to smile, and a genuine smile is a gift that is nearly always returned. A smile can completely change the way you are perceived by others, and a smile can change the way in which you view others. So smile as much as you can.

It is true that there have been few charismatic people that have not first developed confidence. In much the same way, I have never met someone with Charisma who lacks empathy. Charismatic individuals are able to understand how it feels to walk in someone else's shoes. They are sympathetic to the needs of others. They are accommodating and supportive. In the words of the Scout Law, they are helpful and kind.

Recently, a former coworker of mine called me to see how everything was going. It seems he had heard that my mother was ill and wanted to make sure I was doing OK. This demonstrates one of the outstanding qualities that all truly great personalities have: thoughtfulness. I have heard it said that thoughtful is the 13th Scout Law. It is impossible to develop a great personality while ignoring the student seated next to you. Do not be afraid to show your concern for others. Be thoughtful and compassionate. Men are more helped by sympathy than by service. A kind word will give more pleasure than a present. Being thoughtful of others is the one true way of giving of yourself. It is not the gift you send, but the thoughtfulness that your actions demonstrate that endears you to others.

Dare to be thoughtful! Dare to develop self-confidence! Dare to be Friendly! Dare to be kind. Dare to develop a personality that makes people attracted to you! Dare to have Charisma!

Chapter 8

Dare to Give to Others

I hope you have accepted the initial 7 Eagle Scout Dares. If you have accepted these challenges there is no doubt that you will be prosperous. You will have a positive attitude. You will be

> Dare to be help other people at all times.

mentally and physically fit. You will be a man of great character who does his best and is not afraid to try. You are almost a success. Almost you might ask? Why almost? Because no one is a true success until they help others in their journey to the top. **Dare to help others.**

Have you ever gone to the fish market and looked inside a barrel of crabs? It is not necessary to put a cover on the crab tank, because as soon as a crab climbs up on the pile and approaches the top of the barrel, a crab from the bottom will reach up and pull the top crab down.

Don't be a crab. Feel joy at the success of others. Instead of pulling others down, prop them up. You can't help someone else get up a hill without bringing yourself close to the top.

Take this quiz:

1. Name baseball's last five most valuable players.
2. Name ten people who have won the Nobel Prize.
3. Name the last six Academy Award winners for best actor.
4. Name the last 10 Super Bowl winners.

How did you do? Not too well? Don't feel bad. Few of us can remember all of the headliners of yesterday. These are no second-rate achievers. They are the best in their fields. But after a short time their achievements are forgotten by most.

Now here's another quiz. See how you do on this one:

1. List a Scout leader who was helpful as you worked your way toward Eagle.
2. Name a teacher who aided your journey through school.
3. Name three friends who have helped you through a difficult time.
4. Name five people who have taught you something worthwhile.
5. Think of a few people who made you feel appreciated and special.
6. Think of five people you enjoy spending time with.

Easier? Of course. The lesson? The people who make a difference in your life are not the ones with the most credentials, the most money, or the most awards. They are the ones who care. **Dare to Care.**

Dare to make a difference in the lives of those around you. What does it mean to make a difference?

There once was a little boy walking along an ocean beach. The beach stretched for miles, literally as far as the eye could see. Every day, there were millions of starfish dying on the beach — creatures that had been washed up onto the beach by waves, but who had no way of returning back into the water.

The little boy began picking up these small urchins, one by one, and returning them to the sea, thus ensuring that they would live.

An elderly man watched this performance, and as the little boy continued along the beach, the man spoke to him. "Little boy, why are you doing this? Can't you see that there are millions of these starfish dying here in the sun?" What you are doing can't possibly make a difference."

The little boy looked at the man for a moment and then reached down, picked up a starfish and returned it to the sea. "I made a difference to this one," he said. In small ways, every day, you can make a difference. Don't think about what can't be done; rather, focus on what you can do.

> Dare to Care.

As a Scout, you have been schooled to do a good turn daily, and it is very important to look for opportunities to do small things for others with every step that you take. Grand opportunities to change the world don't come to us every day but little opportunities to be kind exist nearly every hour of our lives.

Mother Teresa was once asked why her order was so dedicated to helping the poor. After all their efforts, there were poorer than ever. It did not take Mother Teresa even a moment to respond to this question. She said, "We ourselves feel that what we are doing is just a drop in the ocean. But the ocean would be less because of that missing drop." The troubles facing our world will not be solved by an ocean of a man that solves every earthly problem, rather our world will be made better by millions of people contributing tiny drops. Seize the opportunity during your lifetime to contribute tiny drops.

Honor begins with accepting that what we do, large or small, matters. Every minute of every day you have an opportunity. Seize this opportunity to be the best you can be and to bring kindness to those around you. It doesn't matter what your position is in life. When you die, God is not going to ask you whether you were the SPL, captain of the team or class valedictorian. What will matter is if you seized the opportunities you had to make a difference in the lives of those around you.

> Dare to be kind.

This doesn't mean that you should be afraid to take on life's great challenges. After all, you are an Eagle Scout, like the 38th president of the United States and the first man to walk on the moon. You have the power to achieve greatness. Food shortages, resource shortages, illness and disease affect everyone on our planet. Perhaps you can change the lives of others through some great invention. Can you solve the energy challenges facing the world through your hard work and creativity? Can you help feed the poor? Can you cure disease? Can you positively influence the thoughts and behavior of others with a powerful book? Can you achieve true greatness?

Think about these great men that perhaps few have heard of. It was the vision of a single man, William Wilberforce, who led the abolition of slavery throughout the British Empire. He dared to envision a world without slavery and he lead a 28-year fight that culminated on February 23, 1807, with a vote by parliament to outlaw slave trade.

There is more food and food is less expensive today because Cyrus Hall McCormick revolutionized farming reducing the required labor and increasing crop yields through the invention of the mechanical reaper.

Nick Holonyak developed the light-emitting diode (LED), which proved a simple and inexpensive way for computers to convey information. Others built on his work to develop lights and devices that are 90% more energy efficient than similar devices built on traditional technology.

American tropical disease expert William Gorgas rid Panama of yellow fever in 18 months by implementing measures to control the mosquito population. His efforts also led to a reduction in Malaria. As a result of his mosquito control measures, Gorgas got these diseases in check, which allowed America to construct the Panama Canal, a project that had been deemed impossible by most experts.

Ken House and Randolph Smith developed a small battery powered smoke detector for home use. Over the next 50 years this device was responsible for saving countless lives.

Molecular biologist Alec Jeffreys devised a way to make DNA analysis more manageable by comparing only the parts of the sequence that show the greatest variation among people. His method quickly found it's way into the courts, where it is now used to exonerate people wrongly accused of crimes and to convict the true perpetrator.

Wilson Greatbatch accidentally grabbed the wrong resistor and connected it to a device he was building to record heartbeats. When the circuit unexpectedly emitted a pulse, he realized the device could be used to control a human heartbeat. In 1960, the first Pacemaker was successfully implanted.

Can you be the next Edision, Wilberforce, Gorgas or Greatbatch? A world of opportunity awaits you. Are you prepared to seize these opportunities? As an Eagle Scout you should be. Remember, the Eagle badge is not given to you simply because of what you have done, but it is awarded to you because it is believed that you have prepared yourself to become a leader. If you take to heart the things you learned along the trail to Eagle, there is no limit to what you can accomplish in life. Be a man of accomplishment! If you embrace the 8 Eagle Scout Dares and endeavor in your daily life to demonstrate a positive attitude, do your best, develop intellect, achieve personal fitness, show faith and character, take action and give to others, you can't help but be a success.

Dare to be a success!

Eagle Scout Dare to Soar Pledge

As an Eagle Scout, I will soar,
I will dare to have a positive attitude,
I will endeavor to think for myself,
To be physically strong,
I will work to be a person of great character,
And to be a man of action.
I will be friendly and cheerful,
I will give to others.
As an Eagle Scout, I will dare to embrace the Eagle Challenge, to do my best,
To take upon myself
The obligations and responsibilities
Of an Eagle Scout.
To this, I pledge my sacred honor.

Eagle Scout Minutes

The short stories each contain a special message to the new Eagle Scout.

The Eagle Story

A boy found an eagle's egg in the woods and brought it home. Unsure of what to do with the egg, the boy placed it in the nest of a backyard hen. The eaglet hatched with the brood of chicks and grew up with them. He adapted to the habits of the barnyard chickens that surrounded him. The Eagle learned to walk and cluck like a chicken. He scratched the earth for worms and insects. He learned to drink from a trough. The Eagle grew in size but was content living the life of a chicken.

Years passed and the eagle grew very old. One day, he saw a magnificent bird far above him in the cloudless sky. It glided in graceful majesty among the powerful wind currents, with scarcely a beat of its strong golden wings.

The aging eagle looked up in awe. "Who is that?" he wondered. "That's the eagle, the king of birds," said his friend the chicken. "He belongs to the sky. We belong to the earth -- we're chickens." So the eagle lived his life among the chickens.

As an Eagle you are called to live the life of an Eagle. You are called not to huddle in the barnyard but to soar to great heights. You must decide if you will cluck with the chickens or soar with the Eagles. **Dare to Soar.**

Eagles in a Storm

Did you know that an eagle knows when a storm is approaching long before it breaks? The eagle will fly to a high point in the sky and wait for the winds to come. When the storm hits, it sets its wings so that the wind will pick it up and lift it above the storm. While the storm rages below, the eagle is soaring above it. The eagle does not escape the storm. It simply uses the storm to lift it higher. It rises to new heights on the winds that bring the storm.

When the storms of life come upon you, you can rise above the storms of life by setting your mind toward God. Storms do not have to overcome you, you can let God's power lift you above them. God's power enables us to ride the winds of sorrow, sickness, tragedy and disappointment. It is not the burdens of life that weigh us down, it is how we handle them.

Leave Your Mistakes Behind You

At the end of a bad day, write down your failures and shortcomings on a piece of paper. Then roll the paper into a ball and throw it away. Close your eyes and put the day behind you — you have discarded your mistakes and you are ready to accept tomorrow as a new day. When tomorrow arrives, start it as the first day of the rest of your life, unfettered by yesterday's rubbish.

The Garbage Man

Once there was a Scout named John who was working toward graduating from high school. When John was 16, his parents died in an automobile accident. To support his younger siblings John was forced to drop out of school and look for a job. He applied for a position as a garbage man, but the town would not hire him. A high school diploma was required in order to get a job as a garbage man. So this young man set about collecting aluminum cans, scrap metal, newspapers and rags. He began recycling these items to support his siblings. John turned his recycling endeavors into a business.

After 20 years he had built the largest recycling business on the East Coast. John became the most well-known person in the town and was admired by all as a generous and successful business man. Consequently, one June he was invited to give the commencement address at the high school he had attended.

When John was introduced at the graduation, the principal told the story of how John had been forced to drop out of high school to support his family. The principal wondered how much more successful could John have been if he completed high school?

John immediately addressed this question. He said, "If I had graduated from high school, today I would be a garbage man. It is only because I was not qualified to be a garbage man that I became a success. It is not the degree you have been given that makes you a success, it is what you do with it."

And so it is true as an Eagle Scout. It is not the badge you have received that makes you a success. It is what you do with it.

Reciprocity

Why is it so hard to convince people that if you plant corn in the spring, come fall you will have stalks of corn, and if you plant carrots, at season's end you will never dig up beets?

Such is life. Whatever you sow during your lifetime that is what you will reap, be it sooner or later. Take a little time during your life to plant things that are good, and someday you will reap the rewards of your actions.

Reverence

Showing reverence to God is necessary not only to be a good Scout, but to be a good American as well. The Declaration of Independence affirms that God's existence is a "self-evident" truth. It proclaims God as "Supreme Lawmaker, God as Creator of all men, God as the Source of all rights, God as the world's supreme judge, and God as our Protector on who we can rely."

Our Country was founded on the principal of respect for others, and the Declaration of Independence reaffirms that we all are created equally. Each of us is awarded inalienable rights to life, liberty and the pursuit of happiness. These rights are not granted by the government, but are given by our Creator.

It is important to keep God in a prominent place in your heart. Have reverence for God, and respect the beliefs of others. This is your obligation not just as a Scout, but as a patriotic American.

A Goose Story

Have you ever watched geese flying south for the winter? You never see one goose going it alone, inevitably what you will see is a large number of Geese flying in a "V" formation. Scientists have

91

discovered that as each bird flaps its wings it creates uplift for the bird immediately following. By flying a "V" formation the whole flock adds at least 71% greater flying range than if each bird flew on its own. When people share a common direction and sense of teamwork they can get where they are going quicker and easier because they are traveling on the thrust of one another.

Whenever a goose falls out of formation, it suddenly feels the drag and resistance of trying to do it alone, and quickly gets into formation to take advantage of the lifting power of the bird immediately in front. If we use our good sense, we will stay in formation with those headed in the same direction we are going. When the lead goose gets tired, he rotates back in the wing and another goose flies the point. It pays to take turns doing difficult jobs. The geese honk from behind to encourage those up front to keep up their speed. Even geese understand the importance of encouraging others.

When a goose gets sick or wounded and falls out, two geese fall out of formation and follow him down to help and protect him. They stay with him until he is able to fly or until he is dead, and then they launch out on their own or with another formation, so they can catch up with their original group. Geese are loyal; they know the importance of sticking together in difficult times. Do you have the sense to stand by others like that?

The Brotherhood of Scouting

The following Scoutmaster's Minute is based upon a story told by Thomas Read, Dean of the University of Florida Law School.

Kyoto, Japan, is a city of many temples, among those temples stands a statue somewhat different than its surroundings. It is a statue of two young men, an American Scout, and a Japanese Scout, clasping hands. How it came to be there is a story worth telling.

Some of the worst fighting of World War II was in Okinawa. It was protracted, and bloody, and fought with fierce determination by both sides. In the midst of one of the battles, near the beach, a young American soldier fell wounded. As he lay there, bleeding and in pain, his vision out of focus, and about to lose consciousness, he saw a Japanese soldier standing over him, bayonet at the ready, poised to strike. He said afterwards he did not even know himself why he did what he then did. He was weak from blood loss and blacking out. But he raised his right hand in a familiar sign - the universally recognized Scout sign. Then he lost consciousness, expecting never to awaken.

He did wake, though. When he came to, he was in an American field hospital. His wounds had been dressed. And in his pocket was a note, written in Japanese. Eventually, he was able to find someone to translate the note and this is what it said:

"I could not bring myself to kill a fellow Scout."

The note also bore the name and address of the Japanese soldier who, instead of taking his life, had spared it, and tended to his wounds before moving on.

When the war had ended, the young soldier was assigned to the occupation force. He went to find his savior at the first opportunity. He discovered that the Japanese soldier who had both spared and saved his life had died later in the fighting on Okinawa. But his family had survived, and the American became their friend and helped them in every way he could during his time in Japan. When asked why, the soldier explained what had occurred, and showed the note, which he still kept.

The people were so touched by this story, that they erected a monument which stands in Kyoto today. It is a monument to our shared humanity that in the midst of war and violence, of hatred and bloodshed, two young men found that they were in fact brothers. It is a monument to the ideals of Scouting — that even when thus deeply divided, Scouting is a link that joins us and encourages compassion, mercy, understanding, and peace.

The statue stands among the temples of Kyoto, a monument to the spiritual values of the worldwide movement known as Scouting. It is also a monument to hope — the hope that if we can only recognize our common bonds, the world would be a better place.

Don't Live in the Past/Future

I will live my life today, content in the knowledge that yesterday is done and tomorrow has not arrived. I know that life does not consist of wallowing in the past or fretting about the future. My life is today, and I will make today the best day it can be. Whatever this day offers, great or small, my life is now.

The Solitary Tree

A Scout was invited to visit his uncle who was a lumberjack in the great Northwest. The Scout and his uncle met at the bottom of the mountain, and as the two pursued their way to the lumber camp, the boy was impressed by the enormous size of trees on every hand. There was a gigantic tree which he observed standing all alone on top of a small hill. The boy, full of awe, called out excitedly, "Uncle George, look at that big tree! It will make a lot of good lumber, won't it?"

Uncle George slowly shook his head, then replied, "No, son, that tree will not make a lot of good lumber. It might make a lot of lumber, but not a lot of good lumber. When a tree grows off by itself, too many branches grow on it. Those branches produce knots when the tree is cut into lumber. The best lumber comes when they grow together in groves. The trees also grow taller and straighter when they grow together."

It is so with people. We become better individuals, more useful timber, when we grow together rather than alone.

You Are Here to Make a Difference

There is a story of a man who stood before God, his heart breaking from the pain and injustice in the world. "Dear God," he cried out, "look at all the suffering, the anguish and distress in your world. Why don't you send help?"

God responded, "I did send help. I sent you."

Success

What is success? Success has nothing to do with what you gain in life or accomplish for yourself. It is all about doing things for others. Every day, little by little, gesture by gesture, word by word you have the chance to be a success. Where there is love and effort, success cannot be far behind. Success is living up to your potential. That's all. Wake up with a smile and go after life with reckless abandon. Don't just show up for troop meetings or the game or at school. Bring everything you've got; try your best; have fun. When you have had fun and done your best, you will know what it feels like to be a success.

Trust

Trust starts with respect. You can't trust someone you don't respect. When you play on a team, you need have respect for yourself, your teammates, your leaders and your opponents. When you respect and trust your teammates, when you can rely on them and they'll come through, you have confidence as an individual player and as a team. The only way to get respect from people is to give respect.

Excellence

We are what we repeatedly do. Excellence is therefore not an act but a habit. You should always strive for excellence. But be careful not to confuse excellence with perfection. Excellence is something that you can strive for; perfection however, is God's business.

Courage

Courage is not just a matter of standing up against a bully, stopping criminals, fighting fires or attacking an enemy in battle. The real tests of courage come in everyday life, when we are faced with the choice of expedience versus doing what is right. Abandoning principles to go along with others is easy. Standing against cruelty, thoughtlessness and evil takes a deep, internal strength and personal risk. Are you courageous? Do you have what it takes to stand up for the weak or small? Are you prepared to stand against those who would harm or ridicule others?

When you are next faced with the chance to test your bravery, will you pass the test?

Satisfaction: Be satisfied with what you have

Hand every Scout a piece of paper and a pencil. Now ask each one to write down five things that they are grateful for. Have a few Scouts share their thoughts on what they are grateful for. When they are done, close with this speech:

From now on I would like you to end each day this same way. Reflect on the day and write down five things that happened that you are grateful for. If you learn to focus on what you have, you will come to know that the good things are limitless, and that life has given you enough. If you spend time thinking about what you don't have, you will never have enough.

Troubles

A small trouble is like a stone. If you bring it close to you and place it just before your eye, it will appear large and out of focus. Hold it further away and you can see it more clearly; then you can begin to better understand what you've got. Throw it at your feet, and you can see it for what it truly is, just another tiny bump on the road of life.

Success

Up to a point, your life is shaped by your environment; by your parents, your race, your religion and where you live. But in life there comes a time when you can decide who you want to be. Only the weak blame their parents, their race, God or lack of good fortune for their ultimate fate. You have the power to say, this is who I am today, that is what I will be tomorrow.

Orienteering Through Life

By now, each of you should feel comfortable reading a map and using a compass to get from one place to another. In life, we are also travelers, going from where we are now to where we want to be. How will you get there? Do you have a map and compass to show you the way?

The Scout Oath, Law and Motto are roadmaps that can guide you through life. When you reach crossroads and don't know where to go, ask yourself, "What if I act according to the Scout Oath or Law?" Chances are these guides will point you in the right direction. With the Scout Oath, Law and Motto by your side, you will never be lost on the road of life.

Leadership

What is leadership? True leadership is more than just leading; it is many things that are difficult to define. Leadership is an opportunity to serve others, rather than a chance to be served. It is about pursuing a higher calling. Strong leaders must have character and faith. Character and faith keep leaders driving unceasingly toward their goal. With faith, leaders overcome great challenges.

Leaders are not leaders because they are appointed or elected - they are leaders because they are followed. To earn the opportunity to lead, a leader must have vision. A leader must raise people's aspirations, and energize those being led in pursuit of a goal. There may be obstacles along the way, but somehow, leaders find a way to get things done. Leadership is all about seeing the world as it should be and changing it through character, faith, effort and determination.

Be Strong in Your Beliefs

If there are five cats on a copy machine and one jumps off. How many are left?

The answer: None. Because they are all copycats.

Don't be a copycat. Develop your own sense of right and wrong. Do things because you believe they are the right things to do, not because others do them.

Can You Sleep When the Wind Blows?

A young man applied for a job as a farmhand. When the farmer asked for his qualifications, he said, "I can sleep when the wind blows." This puzzled the farmer. But he liked the young man, and hired him.

A few days later, the farmer and his wife were awakened in the night by a violent storm. They quickly began to check things out to see if all was secure. They found that the shutters of the farmhouse had been securely fastened. A good supply of logs had been set next to the fireplace. The young man slept soundly. The farmer and his wife then inspected their property. They found that the farm tools had been placed in the storage shed, safe from the elements. The tractor had been moved into the garage. The barn was properly locked. Even the animals were calm. All was well.

The farmer then understood the meaning of the young man's words, "I can sleep when the wind blows." Because the farmhand did his work loyally and faithfully when the skies were clear, he was prepared for the storm when it broke. So when the wind blew, he was not afraid. He could sleep in peace.

– Author Unknown

This story illustrates a principle that is often overlooked about being prepared for various events that occur in life. There was nothing dramatic or sensational in the young farmhand's preparations -- he just faithfully did what was needed each day. Consequently, peace was his, even in a storm. A short poem expresses this principle as it pertains to your life:

It isn't the things you do,
It's the things you leave undone,
Which gives you a bit of heartache,
At the setting of the sun.
What are you leaving undone?

Leadership

Harry S. Truman on leadership: How far would Moses have gone if he had taken a poll in Egypt. What would Jesus Christ have preached if he had taken a poll in the land of Israel? What would have happened to the reformation if Martin Luther had taken polls? It isn't polls or public opinion at the moment that counts. It is right, wrong and leadership.

True Religion

In a mountainous area of Italy, four men sat around a fire arguing over which religion was "true." Each believed that his own religion offered the greatest assurance of salvation. They argued and argued but could not find agreement on a single point. An old man sat beyond the group listening but not saying a word. In frustration the four men turned to this elderly man and asked him to try and settle their dispute.

"Kind friends," he began, "at the end of the season when you make your wine, there are many ways for you to take it to be sold. You can take the northern route, which is the shortest, but it is filled with potholes. Or you can take the southern route where the road is smooth, but it takes longer. You can even decide to climb over the mountain, although this route is very dangerous. When you reach the market however, the buyer does not ask you which way you came. He simply asks, "Friend, how good is your wine?"

A Sea of Difference

In Israel, there are two major bodies of water fed by the waters of the River Jordan. The first is the Sea of Galilee, which is full of fish, and is surrounded by lush vegetation and trees. It is a living body in every sense. The other body of water fed by the Jordan is the Dead Sea. There is nothing green there, there are no fish, and the sea is stagnant and dead.

Why is the Sea of Galilee so vibrant and the Dead Sea so stagnant? After all the source of their water is the same. The difference is that the Sea of Galilee overflows; for every gallon of water that flows into the sea, a gallon is given up and passed on downstream. This sea is constantly renewing itself, it gives away as much as it takes.

The Dead Sea, on the other hand, only takes.

It gives up nothing. Water enters the Dead Sea and never flows out; the water there is never cleansed, it stagnates and dies. And everything depending on this water dies also.

People are very like these two different seas. Those that only take bring death and stagnation to those around them, and those that take and give bring energy and life to those around them. I hope that you can be like the Sea of Galilee and share what has been given to you with those around you.

I Am an American

"I am an American." That's the way that most of us put it, just matter-of-factly. They are plain words, those four; you could write them on your thumbnail, or you could sweep them clear across the bright autumn sky. But remember, too, that they are a way of life. So, whenever you speak them, speak them proudly, speak them gratefully "I AM AN AMERICAN!"

Don't Take Yourself Too Seriously

If you want to be a successful leader, don't take yourself too seriously. Some of our most successful presidents have found a way to maintain their dignity, yet poke fun at themselves to make them more human and likeable. Ronald Regan joked about his age, President Taft made light of his portliness, Lincoln spun tales of his awkwardness as a youth. Each of these men had their imperfections, nonetheless, they were all truly great leaders.

Leadership is not just a serious business. It is about making people feel good about themselves and inspiring them into action. It is teaching others that, "I can get the job done in spite of my imperfections. Follow me, and you can too!"

Stay in Control

No one was a more unexpected selection to the 1984 American League All-Star Team than Phil Niekro of the New York Yankees. Neikro had been released
the previous year from the Atlanta Braves at the age of 45. The Braves had thought his career was finished
after a 1983 season in which Niekro had won only 11 games. Niekro could have quit, or lashed out at Atlanta management for abandoning him. Instead, Niekro quietly signed with the Yankees and went on to win 11 games before the All-Star break. "There are lots of things you can't control," he said, "but you can control how you react to them."

Sometimes the difference between winners and losers is that winners are in control.

Ten Commandments of Human Relations

1. Speak to people - there is nothing as nice as a cheerful word of greeting. (Friendly, Kind and Cheerful)
2. Smile at people - it takes sixty-five muscles to frown, only fifteen to smile. (Friendly and Cheerful)
3. Call people by name - the sweetest music to anyone's ear is the sound of their own name.
4. Be friendly - if you would have friends, be friendly. (Friendly)
5. Be polite and cordial - speak and act as if everything that you do is a real pleasure. (Courteous)
6. Be genuinely interested in people - you can like everybody if you try.
7. Be generous with praise - cautious with criticism.

8. Be considerate of the feelings of others - it will be appreciated. (Kind)
9. Be thoughtful of the opinions of others - there are three sides to a controversy; yours, the other person's and the right one.
10. Be helpful - what counts most in life is what we do for others. (Helpful)

It is interesting to note how many of these "commandments" are really another way of stating the points in the Scout Law.

What's in a Name?

Scouts I'd like to tell you about one of the most important lessons I ever learned in high school. During my freshman year my English teacher gave us a pop quiz. I was a good student and had breezed through most of the questions, until I came to the last one: "What is the name of the man that cleans our school?"

Surely this was some kind of joke. I had seen this janitor several times. He was short and heavyset, he might have been close to 50 years old. But how would I know his name? I handed in my paper, leaving the last question blank.

Before class ended, one student asked if the last question would count toward our quiz grade.

"Absolutely," said the instructor. "In your lives and in your careers you will meet many people. All are significant. They deserve your attention and care, even if all you do is smile and say hello."

I've never forgotten that lesson. I also learned his name was Mr. Wilson. Remember, a Scout is Courteous, Kind and Friendly. If you want to exhibit these traits you need to give your care and attention to everyone you encounter in <u>your</u> daily lives.

Winning

A winner is someone who sets goals, commits to those goals, and then pursues these goals with all the ability given to him. It takes courage to be a winner, you need to push yourself to places that you have
never been before. Before you can win against others, you need to learn to beat the "you" of yesterday. You need to focus on doing little things right each and every day.

Leadership

The general was in real trouble. He was facing an enemy army that was bigger and much better equipped. Moreover, he needed food, equipment and supplies and had no money to buy them. It was winter, and the river between him and the enemy was so full of ice that everyone knew it could not be crossed. Everyone that is, except for the General.

This General did not accept the conventional wisdom, and instead led his Army to do the impossible. He put his men in small boats, crossed the river, and surprised the enemy, capturing a thousand men while sending the remainder of the enemy army fleeing.

George Washington knew that leadership is about finding a way to get things done, even when others say it can't be. Many men still wait until the ice is out of the river... or business is better...or conditions improve to take action. But today, as in 1776, the way to win is not to wait for the ice to go, but to cross the river and attack.

Happiness

Think positive thoughts, and don't dwell on the negative ones. Remember the words of Helen Keller: "When one door of happiness closes, another opens; but often we look so long at the closed door that we do not see the one that has been opened for us." She was without hearing or sight yet found a way to be both successful and happy. Happiness isn't what you have or who you are or where you are or what you are doing that makes you happy or unhappy. It is what you think about.

Is Your Jar Full?

A philosophy professor stood before his class and had some items in front of him. When class began, wordlessly he picked up a large empty mayonnaise jar and proceeded to fill it with rocks, rocks about 2 inches in diameter. He then asked the students if the jar was full. They agreed that it was. So, the professor then picked up a box of pebbles and poured them into the jar. He shook the jar lightly. The pebbles, of course, rolled into the open areas between the rocks. He then asked the students again if the jar was full. With a little hesitation most agreed that the jar was now full. The students laughed as the professor picked up a box of sand and poured it into the jar. Of course, the sand filled up everything else.

"Now," said the professor, "I want you to recognize that this is your life. The rocks are the important things – like your family, and your health - anything that is so important to you that if it were lost, you would be nearly destroyed. The pebbles are the other things that really matter like your schooling, your bike and your friends. And the sand is everything else - The small stuff."

If you put the sand into the jar first, there is no room for the pebbles or the rocks. The same goes for your life. If you spend all your energy and time on the small stuff, you will never have room for the things that are important to you. Pay attention to the things that are critical to your happiness.

Set your priorities. Spend time with your family. Exercise. Eat healthy foods. Take time to get medical checkups. There will always be time for other things, but put first those things that are important. Once you learn to handle the important things first you will find everything else falls into place, and these other items will really take care of themselves.

Remember, take care of the rocks first – the things that really matter. The rest is just sand.

Take Pride in Producing Quality

We've all heard the saying, "Anything worth doing is worth doing well." But how many of us take it to heart? We all have tasks to do, some of which are less enjoyable than others. It's easy to put out the minimum effort, and what is the result? Usually a poor one, one that doesn't last or isn't complete, and one that usually requires additional work later on, work that probably wouldn't have been necessary if a little more time had been devoted to doing a good thorough job in the first place.

Now, think about something that you spent time on -- something that you truly felt was your best effort. Whether it was something you made, a report you wrote for school, a musical piece you mastered, it was, no doubt, something that you took great pride in while working on it and something that you still are proud of today. Take the extra time to be sure that everything you do is done to the best of your ability.

What I Learned From the Railroad

A good friend of mine was a track repairman on the Metro North Railroad. He used to like to say, "If you pay enough attention in any situation, you can learn something." Here's what working on the railroad taught him about life:

1. No matter how hard you try, you can't take your train over the river when the drawbridge is raised. Don't try to do the impossible. Instead focus on what can be done.

2. If you run a red signal, you put your own life and the lives of others in danger. Rules exist for a reason. Follow the rules.

3. Make sure the light at the end of the tunnel isn't an oncoming train. See things for what they really are.

4. As long as you are going past the station, you might as well stop and take on whatever passengers you can. Wherever you go, see the opportunities and make the most of them.

5. If you don't choose to get off at a given stop, you will end up at the end of the line. In life you need to know where you are going if you want to reach your destination.

6. As much as you might be attached to your favorite old engine, sometimes a newer model will get you where you are going much faster. Don't be afraid to try something new.

7. Even if you are on the right track, you will get run over if you just sit there. Take action to accomplish your goals.
8. When riding the train, choose your station and get off the train at the proper time. Destiny is a matter of choice, not a question of chance.
9. As much as you might have enjoyed riding in the caboose, some things outlive their usefulness and we need to leave those things behind. Be forward looking -- don't live in the past.
10. If you miss the express, take the local train and sit back and enjoy the ride. Make the best of bad situations. Find happiness in whatever you do.

Inspirations from Baden-Powell

The following inspirations are based on the words of Baden Powel, I the founder of the Scouting movement:

The Words of Baden-Powell

Be Prepared

The end is character with purpose.

Just like Saint George of Old, the Boy Scouts of today fight against everything evil and unclean.

There is no religious side to the movement; the whole of it is based on religion.

As a Scout, you are obliged to do at least one good turn daily.

You can smile at the rain if you have pitched your tent properly.

Scouts learn endurance in the open, like explorers, they carry their own burdens and 'paddle their own canoes.'

A Scout is 'clean in thought, word and deed.'

The Scout movement is a world-wide brotherhood.

A boy learning what he can as a Scout has a good chance in the world.

Obey the Scout Law.

- B.P.

Honesty

Honesty is a form of honor. An honorable man can be trusted with any amount of valuables with the certainty that he will not steal it. Cheating at any time is a sneaking, underhanded thing to do.

When you feel inclined to cheat in order to win a game, or feel distressed when a game in which you are playing is going against you, just say to yourself, "After all, it is only a game. It won't kill me if I do lose. One can't always win, I will stick to it in case of a chance coming."

If you keep your head in this way, you will very often find that you win after all from not being over anxious or despairing.

And don't forget, whenever you do lose a game, if you are a true Scout, you will at once cheer the winning team or shake hands with and congratulate the fellow who has beaten you.
– B.P.

The Blanket

I often think that when the sun goes down the world is hidden by a big blanket from the light of heaven, but the stars are little holes pierced in that by those who have done good deeds in this world. The stars are not all the same size; some are big, some are little, and some men have done great deeds and some men small deeds, but they have made their hole in the blanket by doing good before the they went to heaven.

Try and make your hole in the blanket by good work while you are on earth. It is something to be good, but it is far better to do good.
– B.P

Belief in God

The atheists maintain that a religion that has to be learnt from books written by men cannot be a true one. But they don't seem to see that besides printed books…God has given us one step; the great book of nature to read; and they cannot say that there is untruth there—the facts stand before them… I do not suggest Nature Study as a form of worship or as a substitute for religion, but I advocate the understanding of Nature as a step in certain cases, towards gaining religion.

– B.P

The Scout Handshake

Our Scout handshake is an ancient sign of bravery and respect. The left handshake comes to us from the Ashanti warriors whom Lord Baden-Powell, the founder of Scouting, met almost 100 years ago in West Africa. He saluted them with his right hand, but the Ashanti chiefs offered their left hands and said, "In our land only the bravest of the brave shake hands with the left hand, because to do so we must drop our shields and our protection."

The Ashantis knew of Baden-Powell's bravery because they had fought against him and with him, and they were proud to offer the left hand of bravery. Be sure to greet other Scouts in friendship by offering the Scout handshake. And when you do, remember that it is a sign of respect and courage.

The Salt of the Earth

Life would pall if it were all sugar. Salt is bitter if taken by itself, but when tasted as part of the dish, it savors the meal. Difficulties are the salt of life.

Be Prepared

Does anyone here know the Scout Motto? That's right, it's "Be Prepared." But what are we supposed to be prepared for? Baden-Powell, the founder of the Scouting movement was once asked this same question by a Scout. His answer was that a Scout should be prepared for, "....any old thing."

That's really a tall order. Life is full of surprises, and we can't be prepared for them all. Or can we? Use your time to learn how to handle an emergency. Think about how you are going to act in a given situation. Develop a strong sense of right and wrong. While we may not know what situation lies before us tomorrow, if we train our bodies, hearts and minds properly, we can truly be prepared for whatever challenges we face.

-B.P

The Wisdom of Chief Sequassen

Growing Deep Roots

Early one spring day, a young brave happened upon Chief Sequassen walking through a cornfield. "It's been a rainy spring," the young brave commented, "it must be good for the crops to have so much rain early in the season."

"No," Chief Sequassen replied, "it may seem good for the crops to get so much rain, but if the weather is too easy, the plants may only grow roots on the surface. If that happens, then a storm could easily destroy the crops. However, if things are not so easy in the beginning, then the plants will have to grow strong, deep roots to get at the water and nourishment down below. If a storm or drought comes along, they are more likely to survive."

"Rough times are an opportunity for all living things to become stronger. You must look at your difficulties as a chance for you to build strong roots, to help you prepare to weather any storms that come your way."

Happiness

Once Chief Sequassen spoke to the tribe about living a happy life.

Everyone has the power to live a happy life. But you must treat happiness like a deer in the forest. It may emerge from the woods to pay you a visit. But it dislikes undue attention. If you chase it, it will run away.

Don't chase happiness. It isn't what you have or who you are or where you are or what you are doing that makes you happy. It is what you think about.

The Dispute

Chief Sequassen was called in to help settle a dispute between two brothers. It seems their father had died and they were arguing bitterly over how to divide his prized possessions. Together, they asked the Chief, would you please divide up my father's inheritance.

Chief Sequassen pondered the situation for a moment before responding. Then he said, "It is not right that an outsider should impose a solution upon a family matter. Therefore, I will ask one of you to divide the land equally, and the other will be awarded first choice as to which half of the property he desires." Often, the best way to solve a problem is involve those that will be most affected by the solution.

Putting Religion into Practice

There was a young brave who was struggling against a very stubborn illness. Chief Sequassen sent him to the medicine man who handed the brave some herbs that were certain to cure the ailment. The brave brought the herbs home and placed them next to his bed. The illness persisted. The illness progressed until the medicine man visited and told the boy to swallow the herbs. Within minutes, the ailment was cured.

The Indians believe that religion is like this medicine. If you don't ingest it, and make it a part of you, it has no value. You cannot simply belong to a religion. You must put it into practice.

The Gifts we are Given

Chief Sequassen decided to go on a long journey. As he got ready to depart, he called together his four sons and presented them each with a gift. In each son's palm he placed a single grain of corn. Then he left, and he did not return to the tribespeople for many years. One day, the wise chief returned and he called his sons together. He asked to see the gifts that he had given them before he left. The eldest son rushed to his teepee and pulled out a small wooden box he had carved specially to hold the little piece of corn. The second son had kept the corn hidden safely under his bed. The third son was unable to find his, so he ran to a storage area, to grab a piece as a substitute for the one he had lost.

The youngest son told Chief Sequassen that he had pondered the gift for a long time before understanding its meaning. Then he took the Chief to the field and said, This is what I did with the gift that you gave me. The Chief looked out at a huge field of corn and said, "Father this will be enough corn to feed the entire tribe this winter."

The Chief knew immediately which son would come to rule the tribe. For you see in life each of us are each given many gifts. What matters is what we do with the gifts that we are given.

Do you know how much is too much?

A young brave approached Chief Sequassen in frustration. "Mighty Chief," he spoke softly, "why am I having so much trouble?"

"You must look at your situation and think about three things that a brave must know if he wishes to survive: what is too much for him, what is too little for him, and what is just right for him."

The Magic Peace Pipe

Chief Sequassen likes to tell the story of the magic peace pipe. Many moons ago there lived a great chief who had three sons. Each of these sons wanted to have the magic peace pipe. When the great chief died he left three pipes for his sons with a note. "My dear sons," the letter began, "one of these is the real peace pipe, the other two are fake." You will know who has the magic peace pipe because the son who owns it will be kind and generous to all people. Each of the three sons spent the rest of their lives being good to others to prove that they in fact had the magic peace pipe.

The chief went on to say, "This is the way it is with religion." The way to show that your religion is true is not to scream or jump up and down. The way to show your religion is true is to live your beliefs every day."

Giving

It was a long standing custom that when the Chief of the tribe entered old age he should divide his horses among three promising braves. Tradition allowed Chief Sequassen to keep his best horse, but the remainder should be divided with half going to the top brave, one third to the second brave and one ninth to the final brave. Unfortunately, Chief Sequassen would have only 17 horses to divide if he kept one for himself. So in spite of his great affection for his best horse, he decided to add his favorite to the group making 18, a number which could easily be divided. Then he gave 9 horses to his top brave, six to a second brave and two to the last. One horse remained, the one that the Chief loved best, and he took it back for himself. The Indians like to say, "When you give away that which you love, it will be returned to you".

Faithful Deer

All the young Indians gathered around the campfire as Chief Sequassen recalled the story of Faithful Deer. When Faithful Deer was a young boy he became friends with Rugged Mountain. The two young Indians were inseparable, and they grew together in wisdom and in strength. The time came when the two were old enough to help provide for the needs of the tribe. So together they hunted wild turkey and game, in summer and winter, during blue sky and rain.

On one winter's day, Faithful Deer was overcome by sickness, so Rugged Mountain went out in search of food alone. Nighttime came and went, but Rugged Mountain did not return. The Chief called together all the people in the tribe and they began to search for Rugged Mountain. For three days Faithful Deer and the others searched in hilltops and valleys, on the plains and near the river, for their lost friend Rugged Mountain. And for three days, no sign of him was seen by anyone. A great storm settled over the area, and the Chief called his people together to stop the search for Rugged Mountain. "Our dear friend could not have survived this long in the wilderness alone," the Chief began. "A storm draws near and we must abandon our search for Rugged Mountain."

Faithful Deer was filled with grief. He could not give up hope that somewhere, somehow, Rugged Mountain was alive. So when nighttime fell he slipped away from the village and continued the search for his friend, alone. The falling snow made each step difficult, but Faithful Deer trudged on looking high and low for Rugged Mountain. After three more days had passed, Faithful Deer heard a cry in the distance. There, beyond the pine trees, lay Rugged Mountain, badly injured and unable to walk.

"How did you manage to survive injured and alone, beaten by cold for all this time," Faithful Deer asked as he embraced Rugged Mountain.

"I never doubted you would come my friend," Rugged Mountain replied. "The strength of our friendship kept me alive."

"So you see my children," Chief Sequassen concluded, "Loyalty carries with it the power of life over death." **A Scout is Loyal**

Too-ka'

Chief Sequassen took the young Indian braves on a trip, to help prepare them to become warriors. Among the braves was a boy named Too-ka'. Too-ka' believed that he was the finest young Indian born since the mighty Chief. Above all, he wanted everyone, especially Chief Sequassen, to be impressed with his wilderness skills.

But things did not go well for Too-ka', as he was paired with a group of braves who burned their supper. "You have ruined our food," Too-ka' complained to the others. Too-ka' next began a small carving project, which ended when he was cut with his own knife. "You bumped me," Too-ka' wined, as he bandaged his hand.

Finally, when night set in, the young braves retired to shelters that had constructed. A strong wind blew and the shelter Too-ka' was sharing collapsed. "You idiots," Too-ka' yelled, "You didn't construct the lean-to properly." The next day, Too-ka' approached the Chief and asked, "Why am I constantly affected by the foolishness of others."

"When bad things happen to us," the Chief explained, "the first place to look for the cause is within ourselves."

The Quest for Knowledge

Twin brothers reached the age in life where they leave the tribe on a quest for knowledge. The braves traveled in separate directions hoping to learn the ways of the world. Walking through the wilderness, the first brave stumbled upon Chief Sequassen.

"What are the people in your tribe like?" the first brave asked.

"Well," Chief Sequassen inquired, "How are the people in your tribe?"

"My tribe is filled with a bunch of miserable people who are always grumpy and unhappy," the first brave replied.

"You will find," the wise Chief responded, "that the people in this area are exactly the same way."

Later, the second brother also came upon the wise old Chief. "How are the people in your tribe," the second brave wondered.

"Well," Chief Sequassen inquired, "How are the people in your tribe?"

"Wonderful!" replied the other brother. "The people in our tribe are always cheerful and friendly, kind, loving and understanding."

"You will find," the wise Chief responded, "that the people in this area are exactly the same way." For you see, the Chief understood that the attitude of the people you meet depends on your own state of mind. If you are happy and cheerful in everything you do, you find the same in others. **A Scout is Cheerful**

The Ceremonial Headdress

A young brave and Chief Sequassen's daughter were in love and hoped to marry. So as was the tradition, the brave approached Chief Sequassen and asked what he could offer for the right to marry his daughter.

The Chief considered the question, and then issued this reply: "My ceremonial headdress is quite old, and needs to be replaced. But it must be made by using only the finest materials, including berries from the agwa bush, feathers from a bald eagle, thread from the ickba tree, and shells from the great ocean. When the new headdress is complete, you may have my daughter's hand in marriage."

So the brave sought out to gather materials for the headdress. But the agwa bush was not yet in season, so agwa berries would be hard to find. Shooting an eagle would be extremely difficult, and finding one of the few very rare ickba trees would also be a great challenge. Finally, the great ocean was far away, and it would take effort to recover the shells.

121

So the brave decided to take a few shortcuts in preparing the headdress. He found berries from the caca bush which he used in place of agwa berries. He used the feathers from a hawk, thread from the nebee tree, and freshwater shells from a nearby lake. When the headdress was done he presented it to Chief Sequassen for his approval. The Chief was very pleased. "I can see you worked hard to prepare this headdress," the Chief began. "Such materials are difficult to collect and you deserve praise for uncovering them so quickly. I am sorry to say, however, that the Chief from a neighboring tribe has presented me with a new ceremonial headdress as a symbol of peace and friendship. I feel compelled to use that headdress now, so I would like you to have the one that you prepared as a wedding gift from me. This beautiful headdress is a picture of your own character, true and loyal from top to bottom."

Imagine how the young brave must have felt! The ceremonial headdress was indeed a picture of his character, and during his wedding ceremony, and throughout his life, when he placed it on his head he would be reminded of his dishonesty, and the shallowness of his character. **A Scout is Trustworthy.**

The Buffalo Stampede

A stampede of buffalo thundered across the plains in the direction of Chief Sequassen's tribe. When the tribespeople heard the sound of the approaching stampede, they began to run in a direction away from the approaching herd. Knowing his people could never outrun the herd, Chief

Sequassen jumped on his horse and headed directly toward the head of the stampede. When the buffalo saw Chief Sequassen approaching they shifted direction and traveled away from the settlement. Thankful tribespeople gathered around to praise the Chief for his courageous response. A young brave wondered about the Chief's action. "It all happened so fast," the brave observed. "How did you decide so quickly that riding into the herd was the best course of action to protect the tribespeople?"

"I did not think," the Chief replied. "I did not have to think. I have considered many times the possible danger a stampede would pose to the settlement, and I made up my mind many moons ago what I would do if this situation ever occurred. When it did, I acted instinctively." **A good Scout is prepared for all possibilities.**

A Bird in the Hand

A young Indian brave was frustrated with Chief Sequassen. He thought the Chief was too old, and he wanted a new Chief. The young brave knew that if he could make Chief Sequassen look like an "old fool" in front of the whole tribe, the Chief would step down. But he also knew Chief Sequassen could be clever at times, so the brave would need a "fool proof" plan. The brave decided to get a small bird and hold it cupped one of his hands. As he spoke, he would hold the bird saying, "Oh mighty Chief, in my hand I have an animal. You are wise beyond imagination. Please tell us what animal it is." He if guessed wrong, the game would be over, as the mighty chief had made a mistake. If he guessed right, the young brave would ask, "Is it alive or is it dead?" If the chief said "dead," the brave would open his hand and the bird would fly away. If he said "alive", the brave would quickly close his hand on the bird and kill it; again proving the Chief less than all-knowing.

The day came when the brave was to put his plan into action. When a lull came in the tribal council's conversation, the young brave jumped up. "Oh mighty, Chief," he said, "I am holding a small animal. Can you tell me what it is?" Chief Sequassen said, "'While I am old, the great spirit has given me great sight to see not only for the tribe, but to hunt well also. And I can see the tiniest feather from the tip of a finch, one of the smallest woodland creatures." The brave then said, "You are right, oh mighty Chief, but is it alive or is it dead?" The Chief grew thoughtful for a moment, and then he said, "The answer to that question, my young friend, is in your hands."

The Dancing Brave

The young Indian brave wanted so much to be like the wise Chief Sequassen. He especially wanted to be able to dance like the old Chief did. While Chief Sequassen had lived many moons, everyone felt he was still the finest dancer in the tribe.

So the young brave went to the Chief and asked to be taught all of the dances. The Chief was very flattered, and seeing that the brave was sincere, he worked very closely with the brave for a whole year.

They both worked hard, and it came to pass that the brave was to perform some dances for the tribal council. After the dancing, the brave was disappointed with his performance. Although he had tried, the results just didn't satisfy him. So he sought out Chief Sequassen and asked him his opinion.

The Chief said, "I have taught you all the steps - and you have learned them well. Now you must hear the music yourself."

Leading the Horse

Chief Sequassen's tribe was spread across vast areas of the northeast, and once a year he would gather with the leaders of various tribal villages in order that they might all share their experiences. Included at one gathering was a younger leader who was having trouble convincing many of his braves to take a more active role in leading the tribe. He was frustrated and was having trouble justifying all his effort, and he was considering handing the tribal responsibilities over to someone else.

Chief Sequassen listened attentively and was sympathetic. He let the younger leader vent his frustrations. "You know," this young leader said, "I've shown them and shown them. I've taught them all the needed skills, but I can't seem to get any of these braves to step up and take the lead. I guess you can lead a horse to water but you can't make him drink."

Chief Sequassen offered a thoughtful reply, "Maybe you're job isn't to lead them. Perhaps your job is to make them thirsty so that they'll find the water themselves....."

The Visitor and the Tracker

Many young braves gathered around the campfire to hear Chief Sequassen tell the story of the Visitor and the Tracker. "Many moons ago a very famous tracker lived among our tribe. Indians from far away would come to learn from this tracker, and he generously shared his knowledge and wisdom with everyone. One day a visitor from another tribe and the Tracker set out to explore the world together. As they wound their way through the wilderness, the visitor was amazed at the Tracker's habit of pausing several times each day to pray.

"'Why do you pray to something intangible? the Visitor asked. How do you know there is a God?'"

The Tracker was very skilled in noticing things and, through the years, he had gained much insight into reading the smallest of signs. The Tracker answered the Visitor in this way:

"I know there is a God when I see the leaves turning yellow. I know there is a God when a trout jumps at a fly, and when grass waves in the dry wind. I know there is a God when clouds shade my head and the stars wink at night."

"So you see," said Chief Sequassen, "the Tracker knew well that God existed, because he had learned to see His footprints throughout the Universe."

Everybody's Canoe

Chief Sequassen likes to tell the story of a young Indian brave who was at work carving a canoe out of a log. As he worked, members of the tribe passed by. Everybody offered the young brave

126

a piece of advice. "I think you are making your canoe too wide," one of the elders said. Wishing to show respect for the advice
of an elder, the young brave narrowed down the canoe. A little later, a warrior stopped by. "I'm afraid you are cutting the stern too full," he said. The young brave listened to the warrior and cut down the stern. Very soon, yet another member of the tribe stopped, watched awhile, then said, "The bow is too sheer." The young brave accepted this advice as well and changed the line of the bow.

Finally the canoe was complete and the young brave launched it. As soon as it hit the water, it capsized. Laboriously he hauled it back onto the beach. Then he found another log and began to work anew. Very soon, a member of his tribe stopped by to offer some advice, but this time the young brave was ready. "See that canoe over there?" he asked, pointing to the useless craft on the beach. "That is everybody's canoe." Then he nodded at the work in progress. "This one," he said, "is my canoe."

The Snake (a warning about drugs)

A group of boys from Chief Sequassen's tribe decided it was time to show the tribal elders that they were old enough to be considered men. By custom, the rite of manhood included living alone for one week in the wilderness. Each boy was instructed to only take a knife with him and come back seven days later and tell of his adventures. One boy, wanting to prove that he was more of a man than the others, decided that he would climb the snow-capped mountains for his week of adventure. Surely, the elders would agree that living in the snow and cold for a week is a hardship only a man could endure. So, the boy walked an entire day across the plains to the foot of the mountains. As he climbed up the mountain, he reached a spot where the snowline began, and as he stopped to rest a snake spoke to him.

"Help me," the snake cried.

"Why should I help you?" the young brave replied, "You are a rattlesnake. You are known to bite and kill people."

"I am cold and almost frozen. Please put me in your warm shirt and take me down the mountain to where it is warm where I can survive," said the rattlesnake.

"How do I know that you are not going to bite and kill me?" asked the brave.

"Why should I bite the person who saves my life?" replied the snake.

"Ok. I do not like to see anyone die. Promise you won't bite me?" asked the brave.

"I promise," replied the snake.

So the Indian boy placed the snake in his shirt and walked down the mountain. As he opened his shirt to let the snake out, the rattlesnake bit him.

"WHY DID YOU BITE ME? You promised you wouldn't bite and kill me!" yelled the young brave.

The snake replied, "You knew who I was when you picked me up. You have nobody to blame for your death but yourself."

Selection of a New Chief

Many moons ago a great Chief was dying and he needed to pick his successor. Since he loved gardening, he decided to use seeds to choose his successor. He called all the young braves to his teepee and gave them each a seed to grow. He asked them to return in the Spring with their plant. Whoever had cared for their plant the best will be named Chief.

One young brave, known among the others as an excellent gardener, could not get his seed to grow. He tried repotting the seed several times but had no luck. At the end of the year, he had nothing to show to
the Chief but an empty pot, while all of the other braves were bringing in huge beautiful plants.

When the great chief saw the young brave with an empty pot, he smiled and said, "It seems you are the only brave who could not get his seed to grow. You will be the next chief."

You see, the mighty Chief knew that honesty is among the most important traits a leader should have. And the Chief had secretly baked each of the seeds so they would not grow. Only one brave was honest and brought forth an empty pot. This brave was the only one trustworthy enough to be the new Chief. **A Scout is trustworthy.**

When Does the Night End?

"How can we determine the hour of dawn - when the night ends and the day begins?" Chief Sequassen asked his young braves.

"When, from a distance, you can distinguish between a bear and a buffalo," one of the braves suggested.

"No" the thoughtful Chief replied.

"Is it when you can distinguish between a pear tree and a grapevine?" another brave suggested.

"No" the Chief answered.

"Please tell us then, what is the answer," the braves wondered.

"It is when you can look into the face of a human being and have enough light to recognize in him your brother," the wise Chief replied.

"Until then, it is night, and the darkness is still with us."

The Horseman

A long time ago, the great Chief Flying Buffalo offered a brave a gift of land. He told the brave that he could ride his horse and cover as much area as he would like, and the chief would give him the area of land that he had covered. Sure enough the brave quickly jumped onto his horse and rode as fast as possible to cover as much area as he could. He kept on riding and riding, beating the horse to go as fast as possible. When the brave was hungry or tired, he did not stop because he wanted to cover as much area as possible. He came to a point he had covered a very substantial area and he got very tired and was dying. Then the brave said to himself, "Why did I push myself so hard to cover so much area? Now I am dying and I only need a very small area to bury myself."

When we chase wealth at the expense of everything else, we end up with nothing.

This minute can also end with the following dialog:

Your life is very much like the life of the horseman. You are given a limited amount of time and while work is important, we should not chase material wealth at the expense of everything else. Take care of your health, make sure you enjoy life, spend time with your family, pursue your hobbies. Life is fragile, do not take life for granted. Be sure to live a balanced life.

Happiness and Spirit

A young brave approached Chief Sequassen and asked, "What is the key to happiness?"

"Well," the Chief began, "many people believe that money and possessions are the main requirements in life, when the truth is all we really need to make us happy is something to be enthusiastic about."

Inspirational Quotes

Quotes about Eagle Scouts

"There is no end to the Eagle Scout Trail."

"To become an Eagle Scout takes a lot of determination. I learned the importance of setting goals and the importance of having the determination to meet those goals and to work hard to get it done and keep working at it until you do get it done."
— J.W. Marriott, Jr. CEO of Marriott International

"Once an Eagle, always an Eagle. It is something that can never be taken away, yet it is a badge that one continues to earn every day."

"I assure you of my own personal appreciation of Scouting as a magnificent experience and form of social and religious commitment."
— His Holiness Pope John Paul II, the Vatican

"Becoming an Eagle Scout is a great accomplishment; being an Eagle Scout is a great responsibility."

"One of the proudest moments of my life came in the court of honor when I was awarded the Eagle Scout badge. I still have that badge. It is a treasured possession."
— President Gerald R. Ford

"Following the Scout Law sounds like a game plan that would give us all a better chance for success in life—and I mean every area of life."
—Zig Ziglar, author and motivational speaker

"I've never forgotten my days as an Eagle Scout. I didn't know it at the time, but what really came out of my Scouting experience was learning how to lead and serve the community. It has come in handy in my career in government."

— Lloyd Bentsen, former Secretary of the Treasury

"I admire the Boy Scouts of America because the BSA has meant finding real solutions to some of the problems plaguing our Country and has kept the faith in what America is and must mean to the world. You show that character comes from one small act at a time, caring for each child as if he or she were our own."

— George Bush, former president of the United States of America

"An Eagle Scout is a marked man. He is expected to stand above all and to exemplify the high principles and values of the Scout Oath and Law."

"In my 30 years working as a Scoutmaster, I have never heard anyone say, "I regret the time I spent in Scouting." Yet I have heard former Scouts say so many times, I won't trade my Scouting experiences for anything."

"Ask any former Scout what, who did not advance to Eagle what was the highest rank they achieved an inevitably you will hear, Tenderfoot, Second Class, First Class, Star or "Life almost Eagle." Rarely will anyone ever say Life, but rather it seems to be

always followed but the words "almost Eagle." I have heard the sound of regret in the voice of many who came so far but yet did not take that final step. But there is no
almost in Eagle Scout. The badge belongs to the few who pursued a goal over many years and who let nothing get in the way of accomplishing that goal."

"In this Country, you don't have to come with a pedigree. You just have to have the principles and the moral and ethical standards, and then you need to have the drive to get things done. All those things you get taught in Scouting."
— Ross Perot

"Being an Eagle Scout means that you took control of your own life. You set an objective, a reasonably complex one for a young man, and you pursued it through difficult times."
— Michael Bloomberg Mayor of New York City

"Becoming an Eagle was the first time in my life that I believed I could lead others. My Scouting experience gave me the confidence to believe I could be a leader, and incidentally, it also gave me the tools to do so."
— Robert M. Gates Secretary of Defense

"The Boy Scouts of America stands for a set of principles. These principles have a lot of staying power. The values you learn as a Scout are like a compass. They can help you find your way through difficult and sometimes unchartered terrain. The principles of Scouting give you a sense of what's important. I feel I owe the Boy Scouts a great deal, both personally and professionally."
— Bill Bradley, former U.S. senator, New Jersey

"I think the character that you learn in Scouting—working together, being honest with each other, being close knit and depending on one another, on our camping trips and doing things—all these things build character in a young man that he takes with him into adulthood and makes him a much better citizen. And that's why Scouting to me has always been an organization I've always wanted to help. I think it's one of the best youth organizations that we have in this Country."

— James A. Lovell Jr., advisory council, Boy Scouts of America, President, Lovell Communications, and mission astronaut, Apollo 13

"Scouting exposes young men to people and experiences that encourage and nurture positive moral values. But we mustn't take Scouting for granted. You can do nothing more important for young people today than to continue, or begin, your support of Scouting. I have never met anyone with devoted Scouting experience who was not a solid citizen, a loyal friend, and a patriot. We need more of them."

— Wallace G. Wilkinson, former governor of Kentucky

"He was a typical Eagle Scout that did his job properly. We go way back."

— John Crosby

Quotes about Eagles

"The eyesight for an eagle is what thought is to a man."
— Dejan Stojanovic

"The eagle has no fear of adversity. Dare to take on challenges like an Eagle, with the fearless spirit of a conqueror!"
— Thomas Mercaldo

"A very great vision is needed and the man who has it must follow it as the eagle seeks the deepest blue of the sky."
— Chief Crazy Horse

"Inside each of us there is an eagle in us that wants to soar, and a hippopotamus that wants to wallow in the mud. Let the Eagle be dominant in your life."
— Author Unknown

"You will never see an eagle of distinction flying low with pigeons of mediocrity."
— Onyi Anyado

"If you associate with eagles, you will learn how to soar to great heights. But if you run with dogs, you will learn how to bark.
— Ojo Michael E.

"In an eagle there is all the wisdom of the world."
— Author Unknown

"Don't quack like a duck, soar like an eagle."
— Ken Blanchard

"And when you reach the place where this understanding overtakes you; that there is no one in the world that will ever love you with the force and power you can love yourself with. That no savior in the form of a spouse or best friend is coming to make you complete and that you are your own savior, your own best friend and perhaps the only savior and best friend you will have, you will soar on wings of eagles and amazing things will happen."

— Adunni Badmus

"Those eagles, like angels, don't distinguish between work and play. To them, it is all one and the same."

— Rebecca Wells

"You cannot fly like an eagle with the wings of a wren."

— William Henry Hudson

"When a storm is coming, all other birds seek shelter. The eagle alone avoids the storm by flying above it. So, in the storms of life may your heart be like an eagle's and soar above."

— Author Unknown

"A believer is a bird in a cage, a freethinker is an eagle parting the clouds with tireless wings."

— Robert Green Ingersoll

"The most amazing lesson in aerodynamics I ever had was the day I climbed a thermal in a glider at the same time as an eagle. I witnessed, close up, effortlessness and lightness combined with strength, precision and determination."

— Norman Foster

"But flies an eagle flight, bold and forth on, Leaving no track behind."
— William Shakespeare

"A friend is like an eagle; you don't find them flying in flocks."
— Anonymous

"The eagle never lost so much time, as when he submitted to learn of the crow."
— William Blake

"When you soar like an eagle, you attract the hunters."
— Milton S. Gould

"Great men are like eagles, and build their nest on some lofty solitude."
— Arthur Schopenhauer

"Only if the dragon and the eagle turn their sights from each other and make room for each other in the world they share, can they reach new and brighter horizons."
— Samuel Berger

"As an eagle, weary after soaring in the sky, folds its wings and flies down to rest in its nest, so does the shining self enter the state of dreamless sleep, where one is freed from all desires."
— Brihadaranyaka Upanishad

"The shaft of the arrow had been feathered with one of the eagle's own plumes. We often give our enemies the means of our own destruction."
— Aesop fable

"When God made the oyster, he guaranteed his absolute economic and social security. He built the oyster a house, his shell, to shelter and protect him from his enemies. But when God made the Eagle, He declared, "The blue sky is the limit—build your own house! The Eagle, not the oyster, is the emblem of America."

— Author unknown

"And there is a Catskill eagle in some souls that can alike dive down into the blackest gorges, and soar out of them again and become invisible in the sunny spaces. And even if he forever flies within the gorge, that gorge is in the mountains; so that even in his lowest swoop the mountain eagle is still higher than other birds upon the plain, even though they soar."

— Herman Melville

General Inspirational Quotes

Friendly
"Saying hi to someone today can result in a new friend tomorrow."
— **Anonymous**

Apathy
"Apathy is the glove into which evil slips its hand."
— **Bodie Thoene**

Confidence
"Confidence, like art, never comes from having all the answers; it comes from being open to all the questions."
— **Earl Gary Stevens**

"Confidence comes not from always being right but from not fearing to be wrong."
— **Peter McIntyre**

Honesty
"The great advantage of telling the truth is that one's so much more likely to sound convincing."
— **Susan Howatch**

"When in doubt, tell the truth. It will confound your enemies and astound your friends."
— **Mark Twain**

"A principle cannot be comprised but only adhered to or surrendered. Honesty is abandoned as much by the theft of a dime as of a dollar."
— **Leonard E. Read**

"Integrity is telling myself the truth. And honesty is telling the truth to other people."
— **Spencer Johnson**

Being American
"Being American is not a matter of birth. We must practice it every day lest we become something else."
— **Malcolm Wallop**

Cheerful
"A positive attitude may not solve all your problems, but it will annoy enough people to make it worth the effort."
— **Herm Albright**

"Reflect upon your present blessings - of which every man has many - not on your past misfortunes, of which all men have some."
— **Author Unknown**

"It is a lot better to hope than not to."
— **Benjamin Stein**

"Happiness is a thing to be practiced, like the violin."
— **John Lubbock**

"Success is getting what you want. Happiness is liking what you get."
— **H. Jackson Brown**

"No situation is so bad that losing your temper won't make it worse."
— **Author Unknown**

Be Prepared
"Dig the well before you are thirsty."
— Chinese Proverb

Troubles
"Nothing lasts forever – not even your troubles."
— Arnold Glasnow

"He who can't endure the bad will not live to see the good."

Clean
"A happy life begins with a clean mind, a clean body, a clean heart and a clean soul."
— Anonymous

"Cleanliness is next to Godliness; Godliness is next to a bar of soap."
— Anonymous

Hate
"I will permit no man to narrow and degrade my soul by making me hate him."
— Booker T. Washington.

Courage
"Courage is not simply one of the virtues, but the form of every virtue at the testing point."
— C.S. Lewis

"Courage is grace under pressure."
— Ernest Hemingway

"The greatest test of courage on earth is to bear defeat without losing heart."
— **R. G. Ingersoll**

Forgiveness
"Forgiveness is a gift of high value. Yet it costs nothing."
— **Betty Smith**

Courteous
"Consideration for others can mean taking a wing instead of a drumstick."
— **Garth Henrichs**

"Speak not against anyone whose burden you have not weighed yourself."
— **Marion Bradley**

"Politeness and consideration for others is like investing pennies and getting dollars back."
— **Thomas Sowell**

"Unless we think of others and do something for them, we miss one of the greatest sources of happiness."
— **Anonymous**

Demand the best
"It's a funny thing about life. If you refuse to accept anything but the best, you very often get it."
— **W. Somerset Maugham**

Destiny
"Lots of folks confuse poor efforts or bad management with destiny."

143

Attitude
"There are no menial jobs, only menial attitudes."
— William J. Bennett

"In the long run the pessimist may be right, but the optimist has a better time on the trip."
— Daniel L. Reardon

Giving
"The only things we ever keep are what we give away."
— Louis Ginsberg

"You received without charge, give without charge."
— Matthew 10:8

Discipline
"Everyone is creative, and everybody is talented. I just don't think that everybody is disciplined. I think that is a rare commodity."
— Al Hirschfeld

"He who lives without discipline dies without honor."
— Icelandic proverb

Don't Give Up
"The word impossible is not in my dictionary."
— Napoleon Bonaparte

Brave
"If you are too careful, you are so occupied being careful that you are sure to stumble over something."
— Gertrude Stein

"Fear is just excitement in need of an attitude adjustment."
— **Russ Quaglia**

"Just because something is impossible doesn't mean you shouldn't do it."
— **Dorothy Day**

Errors
"Mistakes are a fact of life. It is the response to the error that counts."
— **Nikki Giovanni**

Excellence
"We are what we repeatedly do. Excellence, therefore, is not an act but a habit."
— **Aristotle**

Excuses
"Excuses are the nails used to build a house of failure."
— **Don Wilder and Bill Recin**

Expectations
"If you accept the expectations of others, especially negative ones, then you never will change the outcome."
— **Michael Jordan**

"High expectations are the key to everything."
— **Sam Walton**

Facts
"Facts do not cease to exist simply because they are ignored."
— **Anonymous**

Faith
"Fear can keep us up all night long, but faith makes one fine pillow."
— Phillip Gulley

"Faith is believing in things when common sense tells you not to."
— Miracle of 34th street.

First Impressions
"You never get a second chance to make a good first impression."
— Paul A. Kallmeyer

Freedom
"Every generation of Americans needs to know that freedom consists not in doing what we like, but in having the right to do what we ought."
— Pope John Paul II

"When your phone doesn't ring you should ring someone else's."
— Anonymous

"If you would win a man to your cause, first convince him that you are his sincere friend."
— Abraham Lincoln

General
"A man's greatest strength develops at the point where he overcomes his greatest weakness."
— Elmer G. Letterman

"No one can make you feel inferior without your consent."
— Eleanor Roosevelt

"The only thing necessary for the triumph of evil is for good men to do nothing."
— Edmund Burke

"Only a fool tests the depth of the water with both feet."
— African proverb

"Everyone thinks of changing humanity and nobody thinks of changing himself."
— Leo Tolstoy

"One cannot hold another man down in a ditch without remaining down in the ditch with him."
— Booker T. Washington

"The only trouble with Boy Scouts is there aren't enough of them."
— Will Rogers

Correcting Our Mistakes
"Once we realize that imperfect understanding is the human condition, there is no shame in being wrong, only in failing to correct our mistakes."
— George Soros

Getting Things Done
"Tomorrow is often the busiest day of the week."
— Spanish Proverb

"It's amazing how much you can get accomplished when no one cares who gets the credit."

"Sometimes something worth doing is worth overdoing."
— David Letterman

"It is easy to sit up and take notice. What is difficult is getting up and taking action."
— Al Batt

"My view is that to sit back and let fate play its hand out and never influence it is not the way man was meant to operate."
— John Glenn

Goals
"Setting the goal is not the main thing. It is deciding how you are going to achieve it and staying with that plan."
— Tom Landry

"When you reach for the stars, you might not get one, but you won't come up with a handful of mud either."
— Leo Burnett

Do it Right
"There are no shortcuts to any place worth going."
— Beverly Sills

Helpful
"No one can sincerely try to help another without helping himself."
— Anonymous

"Great opportunities to help others seldom come, but small ones surround us every day."
— Anonymous

"The people who make a difference are not those with money, credentials, or special skills; rather the people who make a difference are the ones with the concern."
— Anonymous

Know Yourself

"He who knows others is clever; he who knows himself is enlightened."
— **Lao-Tzu**

Make the World a Better Place

"In every community there is work to be done. In every nation there are wounds to heal. In every heart there is the power to do it."
— **Marianne Williamson.**

Industrious

"Look at a day when you are supremely satisfied at the end. It's not a day when you lounge around doing nothing. It's when you've had everything to do, and you've done it."
— **Margaret Thatcher**

Hope

"The difficult takes long - the impossible takes a little longer."
— **Art Berg**

"Sometimes you have to look reality in the eye and deny it."
— **Garrison Keller**

"Some of the world's greatest feats were accomplished by people not smart enough to know they were impossible."
— **Doug Larson**

"He who gains a victory over other men is strong, but he who gains a victory over himself is all-powerful."
— **Confucius**

"A loud voice cannot compete with a clear voice even if it's a whisper."
— **Barry Kaufman**

"Only through resistance does one gain strength."
— **Anonymous**

"He knows not his own strength that has not met adversity."
— **Ben Jonson**

"We ourselves feel that what we are doing is just a drop in the ocean. But the ocean would be less because of that missing drop."
— **Mother Teresa**

"The truth of the matter is that you always know the right thing to do. The hard part is doing it."
— **Norman Schwarzkopf**

"Good habits are just as hard to break as bad ones."
— **Colleen Mariah Rae**

"The first rule of holes; when you're in one, stop digging."
— **Molly Ivins**

"Never assume the obvious is true."
— **William Safire**

Doing Little Things
"Doing little things with a strong desire to please God makes them great."
— **Saint Francis de Sales**

Kind

"It is not genius, nor glory, nor love that reflects the greatness of the human soul; it is kindness."
— Henri-Dominque Lacordaire

"Genuine goodness is threatening to those at the opposite end of the moral spectrum."
— Charles Spencer

"If you want others to be happy, practice compassion. If you want to be happy, practice compassion."
— Dalai Lama

"Kindness can be its own motive. We are made kind by being kind."
— Eric Hoffer

"Two important things are to have a genuine interest in people and to be kind to them. Kindness, I've discovered, is everything."
— Anonymous

"Kind words can be short and easy to speak, but their echoes are truly endless."
— Mother Theresa

Leadership

"As a leader you must never tell people how to do things. Tell them what to do and they will surprise you with their ingenuity."
— General George S. Patton

"Leadership is about determining what needs to be done and finding a way to do it."
— Abraham Lincoln

"Rank does not confer privilege or give power. It imposes responsibility."
— Peter Drucker

"Good leaders are like baseball umpires; they go practically unnoticed when doing their jobs right."
— Bryd Baggert

"Ordinary leaders believe leading is about organizing and running meetings. Extraordinary leaders know leading is about pursuing a higher calling."
— Anonymous

"Leadership is a potent combination of strategy and character. But if you must be without one, be without the strategy."
— General H. Norman Schwartkopf

"The essence of leadership is that you have to have vision. You can't blow an uncertain trumpet."
— Theodore Hesburgh

"Leadership is the opportunity to serve. It is not a trumpet to call self-importance."
— J. Donald Walters

"A leader's role is to raise people's aspirations for what they can become, and to release their energies so they will try to get there."
— David Gergen

Limits
"Most successful football players not only accept rules and limitations but, I believe, they need them. Players

are free to perform at their best only when they know what the expectations are, where the limits stand. I see this as a biblical principle that also applies to life, a principle our society as a whole has forgotten: you can't enjoy true freedom without limits."
— **Tom Landry**

Loving others
"Getting other people to like you, is simply the other side of liking them."
— **Anonymous**

Loyal
"During good times it is easy to support family and friends. Loyalty is standing by others in difficult times."
— **Anonymous**

Laughter
"A day without laughter is a day wasted."
— **Groucho Marx**

Making of a Team
"One man can be a crucial ingredient on a team, but one man cannot make a team."
— **Kareem Abdul-Jabbar, NBA Center**

Winners
"It's not true that nice guys finish last. Nice guys are winners before the game even starts."
— **Addison Walker**

"The minute you start talking about what you're going to do if you lose, you have lost."
— **George P. Schultz**

"You are never a loser until you quit trying."
— Mike Ditka

"To be a great champion you must believe you are the best. If you are not, pretend you are."
— Muhammad Ali

"The greatest test of courage on earth is to bear defeat without losing heart."
— R. G. Ingersoll

Making things Happen
"The best way to predict the future is to create it."
— Peter F. Drucker

"If you are still talking about what you did yesterday, you haven't done much today."
— Anonymous

"A sense of humor is part of the art of leadership, of getting along with people, of getting things done."
— Anonymous

Sharing
"The miracle is this – the more we share, the more we have."
— Leonard Nimoy

Mistakes
"Mistakes are a part of the dues one pays for a full life."
— Sophia Loren

Obedient

"It is easy to obey your parents when you believe they are correct; however, honor only comes from doing their will when you are in conflict with it."
— Anonymous

Overcoming Obstacles

"You can do anything you want to do if you really put your heart, soul, and mind into it."
— Joe Frazier, Heavyweight Champion

"Kites rise highest against the wind, not with it."
— Winston Churchill

Patience

"Be patient with others, but most of all be patient with yourself."
— Anonymous

"In any contest between power and patience, bet on patience."
— W. B. Prescott.

Putting your best foot forward

"Putting your best foot forward at least keeps it out of your mouth."
— Morris Mandel

Persistence

"Being defeated is often a temporary condition. Giving up is what makes it permanent."
— Marilyn vos Savant

Power

"True power is knowing that you can but you don't."
— Anonymous

Problems
"A problem is a chance to do your best."
— **Duke Ellington**

Respect
"Teach respect for all and fear for none."
— **John Wooden, College Basketball Coach**

Reverent
"One filled with joy preaches without preaching."
— **Mother Theresa**

"Pray as though everything depends on God. Work as though everything depends on you."
— **Saint Ignatius**

Saying Sorry
"Never ruin an apology with an excuse."
— **Kimberly Johnson**

Solving Problems
"There is a time in the life of every problem when it is big enough to see, yet small enough to solve"
— **Michael Leavitt**

Paying Attention
"I think the one lesson I have learned is that there is no substitute for paying attention."
— **Diane Sawyer**

The Importance of Hard Work
"Nothing worthwhile or long lasting can be achieved without hard work. During my Princeton days, my father once told me, "Son, when you're not out there

practicing, someone else is. And when you meet that person, he is going to beat you."
— Bill Bradley, Professional Basketball Star

Thrifty
"The people of this world discard enough food and clothing to feed and clothe everyone in need on this planet."
— Anonymous

You have to try
"You may be disappointed if you fail, but you are doomed if you don't try."
— Beverly Sills

Trustworthy
"Before you can be trusted with great things, you must prove yourself trustworthy with lesser ones."
"He who does not prevent a crime when he can, encourages it."
— Anonymous

Perseverance
"Inside of a ring or out, ain't nothing wrong with going down. It's staying down that's wrong."
— Muhammad Ali

Wisdom
"To acquire knowledge one must study; but to acquire wisdom one must observe."
— Marilyn vos Savant

"The art of being wise is the art of knowing what to overlook."
— William James

"Wisdom requires seeing things two ways, how you want them to be, and how they have to be."
— **Anonymous**

"It takes considerable knowledge just to realize the extent of your own ignorance."
— **Thomas Sowell**

"Wisdom too often never comes, and so one ought not to reject it merely because it comes late."
— **Felix Frankfurter**

"In life all good things come hard, but wisdom is the hardest to come by."
— **Lucille Ball**

Success
"No one ever excused his way to success."
— **Dave del Dotto**

"The greatest successes have been for those who have accepted the heaviest risks."
— **Anonymous**

"Successful people are very lucky. Just ask any failure."
—**Michael Levine**

"Success is a state of mind. If you want success, start thinking of yourself as a success."
— **Anonymous**

I am the Eagle

I am the eagle. Since the beginning of time, man has used me and my brothers as a symbol of royalty, power, victory and valor. My strength and courage has inspired men through the ages.

Ancient man looked upon me as an inveterate enemy of serpents. They saw battle between the sun and clouds as battles between an eagle and a serpent.

The ancient Assyrians associated me with Ashur, the great sun god. I was awed and worshipped for my majestic beauty. In the Assyrian myths, I was a symbol of storms and lightning and the god who carried souls to Hades.

In India and Babylon I was the symbol of fire, of wind and storms, and the bringer of immortality.

In the golden age of Greece, I was a symbol of victory and supreme spiritual energy. I was the sacred bird of Zeus, the ruler of all gods. The Greeks represented me with wings outstretched holding a serpent in my claws. Thus I represented the triumph of good over evil.

In Rome, I was the symbol of Jupiter, the supreme God. The Romans saw me as a symbol of victory. As the Roman legions conquered the world, they marched under the standard of the eagle, with outstretched wings. The silver eagle was the symbol of the republic and the Roman Empire used the golden eagle as its symbol. I became the personal emblem of the Caesars, representing supreme authority. In the Middle Ages, I became the symbol of Germany. And, as falconry flourished in Europe, only kings were allowed to hunt with an eagle.

The rise of Christianity brought me still more honor. To the early Christians, the eagle was the symbol of ascension. This was due to the strong flight of the eagle with its gaze fixed on the sun. In early icons I was known as the symbol of Saint John, the Evangelist.

In the 19th century, French troops under Napoleon conquered Europe under the symbol of the eagle. Many French soldiers gave their lives to protect the golden eagle which supported the French flag on the battleground.

On June 20, 1782, I became the symbol of a new country. Because of my courage and beauty, I was chosen to symbolize the new United States of America. The eagle became a prominent feature of the seal of state of the new republic.

From this early beginning, I have been used in many ways to symbolize the ideals of this Country. Several states have the eagle on their state flags. You can find me on the coins of America from the beginning to present day.

I have a prominent place in America, as in ancient Rome, as a symbol of power and authority. The emblems of the President, Vice President, several members of the President's cabinet and most branches of the armed forces center on the eagle. From the god of the Assyrians, to the symbol of the Caesars, to the emblem of this Country, it was thus fitting that the eagle has a part in the most momentous achievement of man. The Apollo XI crew chose "Eagle" as the name for the lunar module that was to make history. And the words of Eagle Scout Neil Armstrong, "... Houston, Tranquility Base here, the EAGLE has landed.", and man was on the moon.

In 1911, following tradition as old as man himself, the Boy Scouts of America chose the eagle to symbolize the very highest in achievement. Through all of history, I have been the symbol of man's best, now the eagle is the symbol of Scouting's best. You are the Eagle!

The Eagle Scout Charge

The Boy Scouts of the world constitute one of the most wholesome and significant movements in history, and you have been counted worthy of this highest rank in its membership. All who know you rejoice in your achievement.

Your position, as you well know, is one of honor and responsibility. You are a marked man. As an Eagle Scout, you have assumed a solemn obligation to do your duty to God, to your Country, to your fellow Scouts and to mankind in general. This is a great undertaking. As you live up to your obligations, you bring honor to yourself and to your brother Scouts. To falter would bring discredit, not only to you, but to your fellow Eagles. Keep your ideals high and your honor bright.

Your responsibility goes beyond your fellow Scouts -- to your Country and your God. America has many good things to give, but these good things depend on the qualities of her citizens. You are prepared to help America in all that she needs most. She has a great past, and you are here to make her future greater. You are charged to be a leader, and to strive toward the best. Lift up every task you do and every office you hold to the high level of service to God and your fellow man. We have too many who use their strength and their intellect to exploit others for selfish gains. You are charged to be among those who dedicate their skills and ability to the common good. Live and serve so that those who know you will be inspired to the highest ideals of life. Build America on the solid foundations of clean living, honest work, unselfish citizenship and reverence